SPORTS PARENTING

Charleston, SC
www.PalmettoPublishing.com

Sports Parenting
Copyright © 2022 by Bill Schillings

TXu2-293-166

All rights reserved

No portion of this book may be reproduced, stored in a retrieval system, or transmitted in any form by any means–electronic, mechanical, photocopy, recording, or other–except for brief quotations in printed reviews, without prior permission of the author.

First Edition

Paperback ISBN: 979-8-8229-0205-3
ebook ISBN: 979-8-8229-0206-0

SPORTS PARENTING

Creating an environment for success ...without going Bat Sh*t Crazy

BILL SCHILLINGS

Table of Contents

Foreword	i
Preface	iii
Introduction: My Dad's Approach	ix

Chapter 1: Why Is Sports Parenting So Hard?
(Inclinations vs. Effectiveness)

Good Intentions	1
Natural Inclinations	4
The Dilemma	8
What Now?	12

Chapter 2: How Do I Coach My Kid?
(Plans vs. Principles)

Team Leaders	15
Developing Independence	18
Risking Freedom	23
What's the Plan?	26

Chapter 3: How Do We Choose the Right Coach/Program? (Form vs. Substance)

Coaching Moments	31
Psychological Contracts: Pros or Coaches?	35
What to Look For	38
Tennis Pros and Car Mechanics	43

Chapter 4: How Do "We" Get to the Next Level?
(Outcome vs. Process)

Practicing with Intensity	47
Getting to the Next Level	51

| Realistic Encouragement | 55 |
| The Word *We* | 61 |

Chapter 5: What Should I Know about Competition?
(Competition vs. Character)

Character and Wiring	65
Competing and Comparing	69
The Discipline of Character	73

Chapter 6: Do I Have to Be as Intense as the Other Parents? (Sprint vs. Marathon)

"What are the Chances of These Kids Becoming Pros?"	77
Finish Lines	81
Rationalizations and Regrets	84
Ends of the Spectrum	90

Chapter 7: Will This Be Worth the Effort?
(Enablement vs. Independence)

Delusions	95
Potential	98
Responsibility	103
What's the Point?	106

Epilogue — 111

Appendix 1: Terms and Expressions — 116

Appendix 2: An Email from the Dark Side — 133

Appendix 3: Short answers to big questions — 147

Acknowledgements — 151

About the Author — 153

Foreword

I coach tennis, and one of the things I tell our players, a lot, is that I never just say things. If I tell a kid, "Great shot," it was a great shot. I do not dole out compliments insincerely.

When I say that I absolutely loved *Sports Parenting*, and that it should be on every parent's bedside table, you can be sure that I mean it.

Through wonderful storytelling, Bill imparts wisdom that gives parents the tools to avoid the batsh#t craziness that has become increasingly prevalent in youth sports. During the days I was reading this book, I was excited each day to come home and pick up where I'd left off the previous day. I could relate to and appreciate everything Bill describes, and many of his stories made me review my own conduct. And vow to do better.

Sports Parenting will be an invaluable resource in helping parents navigate the often trying circumstances that come with having a child involved in organized athletics. But the reason I say it should be on bedside table of every parent—even those whose kids are not athletes—is that it's applicable to the trying circumstances that come with whatever the child is doing. (I'd even suggest that every child should have it bedside as well, so they can tell their parents when they're screwing up. What kid doesn't relish an opportunity to do that?)

I've known Bill for close to thirty years. Our lunches, where we talk about . . . everything, are a joy. Over the years, when people have sought my help in identifying a great tennis coach for their child, I have not hesitated in answering, "Bill Schillings." He knows tennis inside and out, and he is humble enough, and smart enough, to know that there is always more he can learn. Mostly, though, my recommendation is because I know of his affection and his concern for the kids. It's unwavering. Of course he's making them into tennis players. But that is so secondary to the impact he has on their personal development, their character, the sort of person they'll become. He's the coach you want to entrust your child to.

Parents, not only does *Sports Parenting* belong on your bedside table, but it probably makes sense to keep a copy handy at all times. Then when your child walks off the court after a tough loss, and you're feeling almost as distraught and frustrated as they are, you can flip through the book for some quick wisdom before you launch into your postmatch analysis.

> **Pender Murphy**
> Founder/director of TLA Tennis (an organization providing free tennis programs to people otherwise unlikely to play tennis); former Association of Tennis Professionals tennis pro (ranked as high as 102 in the world); three-time All-American at Clemson University

Preface

This book is my attempt to organize my thoughts on the good, the bad, and the ugly of sports parenting. It is the result of working with and observing the parents I've interacted with as the owner/director of a successful junior tennis academy for over 30 years. It started as a journal for my own purposes, mainly a therapeutic hobby. I claim no title as a sports parenting expert.

But a number of years ago I was having dinner with the Banks family here in Charlotte. Their son, John, was coming to the end of his junior tennis journey and getting ready to play Division 1 college tennis. As we reminisced a bit, John's dad mentioned that some of the sports parenting advice I had shared was helpful to them over the years. He suggested that it might be helpful for other parents if I would write down some of those thoughts. Maybe in the form of a reference book based on common questions that parents ask.

Both of John's parents were doctors, highly intelligent people, and, from my perspective, had been great sports parents who needed little help from me. I was flattered, and a little surprised, to hear that I had said anything on the topic of sports parenting that was of value to them. But since I thought so highly of John's parents, I went home and started thinking about how it might be possible to organize my journals into book form. That was thirteen years ago, and counting—writing a book is easy in concept, but I've found it a little tough to execute.

There have been two voices in my head as I've worked on this. The first is the most powerful and accounts for why this has taken so long. It asks questions like: Who needs more content on any topic in the world of the internet today, particularly one as narrow as sports parenting? What makes you qualified or credible on this topic? Why are you sitting here when you could be outside teaching tennis and making money? You get the idea.

I came close to giving up until about three years ago when I read a book called *The War of Art*, by Steven Pressfield. I learned about "resistance" and how it works against anyone trying to create anything worthwhile. For a more detailed and brilliant exposition of this concept, I highly recommend the book.[1] I also thought often of a favorite line from C.S. Lewis in *Mere Christianity* on the importance of "listening to that other voice, taking that other point of view, letting that other larger, stronger, quieter life come flowing in."[2]

And so I pressed on. As I did, that *other* voice—let's call it the voice of faith—became louder. It pointed out that writing a book would be a win for me regardless of whether it saw life beyond my computer screen, because it would force me to be more disciplined, more focused, and learn how to think clearly. These are against all my natural tendencies. I'm more of a doer than a thinker. Sometimes that *other* voice was bold enough to wonder if this project might

---

[1] See Steven Pressfield, *The War of Art: Break through the Blocks and Win Your Inner Creative Battles* (New York: Black Irish Entertainment, 2002).

[2] C.S. Lewis, *Mere Christianity* (New York: HarperOne, 1952), 198.

benefit someone else, as the Bankses suggested. Maybe this would be an opportunity to connect with parents beyond the everyday routine of clinic drop-offs and lesson-scheduling texts. All that would be nice but, as strange as this may sound, it would likely be unintentional on my part. If there's one thing I've learned from teaching tennis, it's that the most powerful connections happen when you aren't trying, when you are just sharing with no agenda or expectations. Whenever I think I've said something smart, no one seems to remember. But sometimes a student, parent, or even one of my daughters will tell me, long after the fact, that I taught them something that helped, something they applied, something that mattered, something that impacted—and I never remember this, have no recollection at all. These things just seem to happen; we don't get to take credit. Sometimes you just have to do things on faith. Learning to do that has, in itself, been worth the effort.

So, a few thoughts to keep in mind as you read this book.

First, the value in a tennis lesson is never in the twenty smart things the coach thinks they said in the course of an hour. It's in the one idea or principle that resonates with the player. If that happens for a sports parent reading this, then it was worth the time for all involved.

Second, I've learned some great things about tennis, and about life, from people with PhDs. But no one has a corner on the market of common sense. This book is simply a compilation of observations by someone who's been around the world of junior sports for a while. They make sense to me.

Lastly, I've learned through teaching tennis that the how-to approach rarely works. Lists of dos and don'ts are forgotten quickly. Whenever I want a student to remember something, I know an illustration or mental picture has a much better chance of sticking. So just a heads-up: this book is light on lists and heavy on stories.

What follows is my best effort at fulfilling the Bankses request. First, I've listed some of the questions sports parents most commonly ask. Second, as I looked at my journal notes, I noticed there were a number of recurring dichotomies sports parents need to balance. They are:

- inclinations vs. effectiveness
- plans vs. principles
- form vs. substance
- outcome vs. process
- competition vs. character
- sprint vs. marathon
- enablement vs. independence

I've listed the questions at the beginning of each chapter followed by a dichotomy that relates best to that question. The pieces I chose for each chapter roughly follow this theme. The main premise of the book is that *the parents who get in trouble tend to prioritize the first half of the dichotomy over the second or they aren't aware of the need for balancing these dichotomies at all.*

I've included brief responses to the questions at the end of the book in an appendix for easy reference. If you decide to read beyond that, be warned that my anecdotes[3] involve the world of tennis and, occasionally, baseball. However, I think the content would be applicable for parents with kids in any sport and even, in many cases, for parents whose kids are in no sport at all.

So here goes. Do with it what you will.

---

[3] Many of the names used in these stories have been changed, some are the real names used with permission.

INTRODUCTION

"It was only a matter of an inch; but an inch is everything when you are balancing. . . . There are an infinity of angles at which one falls, only one at which one stands."

—G.K. Chesterton

My Dad's Approach

When I was young, my life revolved around baseball. By age eight, I had spent many hours fielding groundballs from my dad in the backyard. I got some bloody lips on the bad hops, but that didn't seem to bother my dad much. This provided one of the early lessons I learned through sports: pursuing excellence takes practice and working through some discomfort. Don't expect sympathy when you get banged up once in a while. My dad established the standards. If he had coddled me, I would've developed a low tolerance for adversity, but since he expected me to work through a challenge, I learned to be tough.

One day after a Little League practice, I got into a fight with one of the bigger kids on the team. The guy beat me up pretty good; I was a pretty scrawny kid. However, due to pride, stupidity, arrogance, or some combination of the three, I got up and kept fighting. After some coaches separated us, I realized that my dad was there the whole time. Apparently, he didn't feel it necessary to save me from that beatdown. When we came home, I overheard him telling my mom how proud he was that I kept getting up and fighting. That brief comment did more to form my character than any lecture he could have given me.

A few years later, I played a Little League game in which I felt I had excelled. I fielded well at shortstop, got a few hits, and to top it off, my team won. Life was good. But in the car on the ride home, I noticed my dad didn't share my enthusiasm. His only comment was that I didn't hustle on and off the field between innings. He didn't elaborate. It was clear, however, that his expectation was that I give 100 percent all the time, focus on the details, and learn to pay attention even when I thought it didn't matter. Once again, one comment from my dad was forming character traits that would impact me into adult life.

I think these early experiences in baseball hard-wired my system. I knew that excellence came at a price. I learned how to work hard, take responsibility, and respect authority. But unfortunately, I also developed a tendency for perfectionism. In my dad's eyes, good was never good enough—at least that's how it felt to me. So that's how I learned to think as well. The combination of all these character traits, some better than others, unconsciously impacted everything I did athletically in the years that followed.

By age thirteen, I found a new sport to play: tennis. My attitude and athletic background helped because within two years I was the best player on my high school team. I went on to play four years of college tennis at a Division I school and even played in the minor leagues of professional tennis for a few years, an opportunity that meant traveling the world for competitions. My Achilles heel was that I was way too hard on myself. Losing a tennis match was a blow to my self-esteem; a bad practice put me in a funk for hours. I really struggled dealing with failure.

One of the last matches I played professionally was in Spain, against a player with whom I was well matched. We were having good points, but I was losing *every* game. My response was to try harder, which was all I knew how to do. As I sat down at my chair at the change of sides, I was down 0-6, 0-5 and working hard to conceal my tears, even though I was twenty-four years old at the time. At that moment I decided to quit and move on to the next chapter in my life. I had no idea what that might be. This was completely out of character and no small decision for a person whose life centered on sports.

The next game I can only describe as an out-of-body experience. I stopped thinking, stopped trying, and just *played*. The next thing I knew the score was 5-5—at which point my usual patterns of thought kicked back in. I started thinking and trying again. Within a few minutes the match was over, I lost the last two games quickly. It's hard to describe how I felt: confused, dejected, lonely. I knew I was physically capable of competing at that level, but my mental wiring, much of which was ingrained at an early age, was getting in the way.

This, I think, illustrates what a tough job sports parents have. Could my dad have taught me to have high standards without being a perfectionist? Could he have taught me character without having been so hard on me? Maybe. But if he hadn't taught me to be hard on myself, I never would have gotten very far in the first place. I think my dad knew that both ends of the parenting spectrum (strict or permissive) had some potential downsides. I suppose he figured the benefits of being tough outweighed the risks of enabling me. I don't think he wasted much time worrying about whether he was the perfect parent. There was no way to predict how I would internalize the lessons he was teaching. He just did what he thought was right at the time based on his own experiences, values, and principles. I'm doubtful he would have had the time or inclination to read a book like this. However, in the end, I'm glad he taught me early in life to set high standards, take responsibility, learn from failure, and work hard—all qualities that have served me well in adult life. But they came at a cost.

It's still, after all these years, tough for me to find the balance between effort and self-acceptance. The patterns of thinking that we form early, I think, tend to stick with us subconsciously our whole lives. And many of those patterns are the direct result of cues we get from our parents. It's never perfect. I think that's one thing my dad accepted. The best we can hope for is a net positive, the good outweighing the bad. Sports parenting is a deceptively challenging undertaking; there's more going on than many people realize, and the stakes are high. *Because it's not ultimately about what your kid achieves in sports; it's about who they become as a result of whatever they achieve.* And how parents interact with their kids has everything to do with who they become. This, I suppose, is why the topic has been so interesting to me in my personal life (as a parent) and professional life (as a coach). The question I've often asked myself is whether it's possible to inculcate good qualities in our kids, often learned through adversity and discomfort, while limiting the collateral damage to their fragile psyches and relationships with us? I think anyone who claims to have a simple answer to this question is either clueless or trying to sell something.

Becoming bat sh*t crazy

When my daughter Kara was a senior in high school, she played tennis for one of the better teams in the area. She had become a fairly good player due to her early and easy access to the sport—her dad owned a tennis academy. She really loved to play the game but, unlike her dad, didn't care that much about competing. Due to my exposure to some overinvolved tennis parents over the years, I made a conscious effort *not* to engage in certain types of behavior. I didn't project my own hopes or vision on her. I rarely coached her, leaving that task to other coaches at our academy. When we did go to hit tennis balls, I was particularly careful not to offer too much advice. I wanted to be her dad, not her coach. I looked at our time on the court as an opportunity to provide a fun practice session and a way for us to spend quality time together. Lastly, I reminded myself never to let myself get too invested in her results on a tennis court.

Since my work schedule conflicted with her tennis matches, I rarely attended, which was all just as well—she didn't need me there anyway. But one day I came home early and she needed a ride home. Her big sister Kristin and I went over to pick her up. Kara was near the end of a challenge match, where players compete for position on the team. She and her teammate/opponent were the last two players on the court. The coach was nowhere to be seen. Without conscious thought, my worst instincts surfaced. I immediately started to evaluate all aspects of the match and became emotionally invested. Back when I was in her shoes as a senior in high school, my whole world revolved around winning challenge matches and being #1 on the team, so to me this was a very, very big deal. It looked as though Kara had won the first set and they were heading towards the end of the second. Crunch time.

I read the body language, attitude, and behavior of the two girls and didn't like what I saw. Kara was being her usual sportswoman-like self: good attitude, giving her best effort, respectful of her opponent. The other girl couldn't have been less so. She seemed to question every line call, kept banging her racquet on the ground after losing points, generally looked miserable, and was, in my view, being disrespectful to Kara. This was pushing just about every button I had as a player, coach, and parent.

Kristin and I were still in the front seat of my car, as if we were at a drive-in movie. I remember glancing over at her, assuming she would be getting just as worked up as I was. She was calmly reading a book, waiting patiently until we could go home and eat dinner. I asked her if she had any idea what was happening out there with Kara. Did she have any opinion about the bitchy attitude of her sister's opponent? Kristin casually replied, "Dad, Kara's above that stuff," and returned to her book. When I glanced back to the court, the girls were shaking hands. I could tell by the other girl's demeanor and the way she stormed off that she had lost. Moments later, Kara bounced into the back seat as if nothing of importance had just taken place. I felt like I was in an alternate reality. Who were these teenage girls in my car? How were we in the same family? Had we all just witnessed the same thing? I was angry at Kara's opponent, frustrated with the absent coach, happy for Kara, and confused at how my daughters didn't feel all these same emotions. They were completely unfazed. I tried to pull myself together and somewhat calmly asked Kara how she felt about the match. She said it was "fine," that the other girl was a bit "cranky," and that she was "like that a lot." No big deal.

As we drove home, I realized I had become, for those few moments, my worst fear as a sports parent: emotional, obsessive, self-absorbed, and irrational. Fortunately, I think that was my only slip up during those years, and thankfully there was no damage done. After all, the only person to suffer that day was me and perhaps Kara's opponent. But I do think it's a good illustration of how easily we all can lose perspective as parents, especially if we project our own "stuff" on our kids as they play sports. I've met many parents who, after exposure to *other* sports parents, have commented how "crazy" or "dysfunctional" or "pathological" (their words) those *other* parents can be. But we don't always sense or acknowledge tendencies in this direction ourselves. No one sets out to be a batsh*t crazy sports parent.[1] Sometimes it just happens.

---

[1] Shout-out here to my friend John for providing this very helpful term to describe the parenting style I'm talking about. I, of course, would never use such salty language of my own volition.

Chapter 1

Why Is Sports Parenting So Hard?

(Inclinations vs. Effectiveness)

*"It ain't what you know that gets you in trouble.
It's what you know for sure that just ain't so."*

—Mark Twain

Good Intentions

Sammy was a precocious and talented kid. By the age of twelve, he was winning most of the tournaments he played and was highly ranked nationally. He was bright, quick-witted, and loved to be the center of attention. He did, however, have a bit of a mischievous streak. I had to keep a close eye on him during clinics for fear he would antagonize the other kids just for the fun of it. When Sammy was on the court, everyone knew it. Some people loved him, others not so much.

Most of Sammy's personality traits applied to his dad, Tom, in exponential proportion. Depending on your perspective, Tom was either lovably gregarious or hopelessly obnoxious. He was a poster child for the parental habit of being around *all the time.* He seemed to know everything about everybody, and he knew everybody. One of his favorite lines was, "It must be great to see me today." I found this funny at first, because I thought he was kidding. Over time, though, I got the feeling he really meant it. Tom was into the details—tournament schedules, match results, rankings, and tactics—and often hand-copied the draw sheets from tournaments (this was the days before the internet) in order to study Sammy's potential opponents. I often thought that Tom enjoyed being around tennis a bit too much; it was as if he was reliving his childhood through Sammy and his buddies. Although I was fairly new to coaching high-level juniors at the time, I felt fairly confident coaching Sammy. I had no idea what to make of his dad.

At that time my youngest daughter was still crawling around in diapers, and I knew I needed to balance my time between work and family. So, in a meeting for the parents of kids in our program, I announced that I wouldn't take calls at my house from parents (no cell phones back then). Tom didn't seem pleased. Our moment of truth came a year or so later, when Sammy attended a weekend training center for promising juniors I had agreed to run for the United States Tennis Association (USTA). That Sunday evening, I was finally enjoying a few moments with my family after my usual full week of teaching plus the weekend running the USTA camp. My home phone rang—it was Tom.

He had a number of issues to discuss. In particular, he was upset about who I had scheduled Sammy to play at the training center. Tom felt that the opponents I assigned weren't challenging enough for a player at Sammy's advanced level. This is a complaint I had learned you hear often working with the parents of high-level juniors. Tom made it clear that he was considering taking Sammy out of my junior program and firing me as his coach. I took this as a threat intended to manipulate me to extend preferential treatment to Sammy in the future. As he continued, my patience with the conversation reached an end. I told Tom that he should do what he felt was right and hung up.

I didn't see Sammy again for five years. We met randomly at a tournament, and he needed a ride from one of the remote sites back to the main park. We had always gotten along well, and spending those few minutes with him was like reconnecting with an old friend. Sammy was not doing nearly as well in tennis as he had in his younger days. He hadn't grown enough physically to compete in the 18-and-under division, but he still had amazing talent—great hands, as we call it in the business. I knew the expectations resulting from his early successes combined with the challenge of being raised in an environment that centered on his tennis had to be burdensome. It seemed that his enthusiasm for tennis was gone. He just wasn't the same precocious, energetic kid anymore. He looked fragile; he had a tennis elbow wrap for his arm and a brace for his knee. He reminded me of the old guys you see playing at the public park on weekends. It was a bittersweet meeting. I missed the fun-loving, rambunctious kid I remembered. It was the last time our paths crossed.

Though he seemed a bit odd at the time, I suppose Tom had Sammy's best interests at heart. He was doing what seemed right to him based on his own personality, beliefs, and life experience. However, regardless of his intentions, I don't think Tom's sports parenting style turned out to be a net positive for Sammy.

Natural Inclinations

I know that I am being tough on Tom, maybe unfairly so. I have no corner on the market when it comes to raising kids, and it's not my place to judge anyone. I do think, however, that Tom's story is a good place to start a book on sports parenting, because I think we all, as parents, have some of Tom in us. I've never met a parent who intentionally tries to make it less likely for their kid to succeed in sports. But I see it happen all the time, because parents operate based on their natural inclinations (what feels right to them) and their own agendas. Sometimes that's constructive; other times it can be dysfunctional. For example, there are four parental inclinations Tom exemplified that, in my opinion, led in the wrong direction. I've seen them all frequently over the years, in myself as well as in others.

The most common inclination is to ENABLE your child. In Tom's case, he felt he needed to be involved in the details of Sammy's athletic life—recording match results, analyzing opponents, scheduling tournaments, analyzing practices, calling the coach on Sunday nights, and so on. I'm sure he rationalized that he was being supportive by making things easier for Sammy. The truth was that most of those details could have been handled by Sammy, because they represented opportunities for him to learn independence, discipline, personal responsibility, and work ethic—all crucial character traits for athletes. Tom was enabling Sammy in the short term instead of thinking about what was best for him in the long term.

Another inclination parents often have is to EVALUATE. Essentially, this is an issue of control. Parents often feel that the more they evaluate the better they can control the outcome. The question is where to draw the line. How much oversight is healthy, and at what point does it get counter-productive? In Toms' case, he acted as if his job was to evaluate who Sammy practiced against, when and how Sammy was playing, what Sammy's draw was in the next tournament, and so on. The reality was that most of those things were out of Tom's control anyway. It would have been more productive to periodically check in with Sammy's coach, observe occasional practices, watch some matches at tournaments, and monitor how Sammy managed his time—none of which required the amount of effort and attention Tom was putting in. But, as I've experienced myself many times, giving up the illusion of control is not something that comes easy in parenting.

Parents inclined toward evaluation often have unreasonable EXPECTATIONS as well. It seemed to me that Tom assumed Sammy's success in his early years would continue indefinitely. When that kind of expectation gets projected onto kids, the pressure is incredibly high. This usually results in kids getting so stressed that they rebel, quit, or ignore their parents altogether. Sports are like the stock market: past performance is no guarantee of future results. When parents learn to focus less on outcomes and more on process, their kids tend to play better, which, ironically, produces better outcomes. If I had to choose one concept that is key to success in sports it would be that. More about this later.

The last inclination Tom had was ENJOYMENT. He just loved to be around tennis, and Sammy's success gave him the chance to do that. It was clear there was no place he would rather be than in the world of junior tennis. Although there is nothing inherently wrong with enjoying sports with your kid, Tom put his own goals, dreams, and passion for tennis ahead of Sammy's. I think he enjoyed being around tennis so much that he didn't realize this. This is an easy mistake to make, especially for parents who have kids who are successful at an early age. Unfortunately this usually leads to over-involvement on the parent's part, which rarely ends well in the long run.

By chance, I ran into Tom years later at a golf/tennis pro-am event. Our meeting was brief and unexpected, but he seemed genuinely glad to see me. That surprised me, considering our differences back when I was coaching Sammy. Tom said I was a good man and had character because I didn't compromise my principles. Maybe, at some level, he realized he had made some mistakes in parenting Sammy during his junior tennis days. But unfortunately, by that time the damage was done. I said thanks and we parted ways amicably.

As I look back on my own experience as a parent, I think about how challenging a balancing act it was at every stage. I wanted to protect my kids but still give them freedom. I wanted to control their environment so they succeeded but also build their character, which is most often achieved by allowing them to fail. I understood Tom better as I got further down the road parenting my own kids. I recognized many of the same inclinations in myself. My instincts often were at odds with my long-term goals. It's hard to know when to push and when to trust. I don't think parents ever get a pass on dealing with this dynamic. It's part of the job. And the environment of junior sports can make that job more challenging due to the emotional attachment we assign to sports in our culture. Some sports parents succeed in finding the right balance, some don't, and some aren't conscious of the need to strike a balance at all. The parents I really worry about are the ones who fall into that last category.

The Dilemma

Parents with kids who show promise early on often struggle to recognize the need for balance. An extreme example of this would be the case of the dad of a talented little boy who was in our program a number of years ago. He would bring his son early and feed him balls before clinic started. This didn't, in itself, concern me. I did notice, however, that the dad would fire a constant stream of corrections and instructions at his son after almost every ball. The mood was always intense, as if he were training a professional athlete. This struck me as particularly unusual because the kid was eight. It was hard for me to watch, since I believe that kids need more positive than negative reinforcement, particularly at that early age when it's so important that kids associate sports with having fun. The boy was already having behavior issues on the court, both at our clinics and in tournament play. One day I got a call from the dad. Apparently his son had gotten into an altercation at a tournament, and the state tennis association had suspended him from tournaments for a few months. The phone call was to ask my opinion on the fairness of the suspension. Throughout our conversation, it was clear that the dad's main concern was that his kid was not going to be allowed to play tournaments. He was so blinded by his aspirations for his son's tennis that he couldn't see the real issue. His kid was becoming a psychological mess and had behavior problems that needed to be addressed immediately. Much of this was due to the dad's approach to sports parenting. My concern was that he was going to derail the train before it left the station. I told him the suspension was a great opportunity for his son to learn life lessons and that was more important than whatever suspension he faced. Shortly thereafter, the dad took his son out of our program. It was pretty clear we had philosophical differences that would not be easily resolved.

Imagine this from a kid's perspective. Within the family he can do nothing right (constantly being pushed and evaluated), but outside the family he can do no wrong (always protected from the consequences of bad behavior). I will leave it to the psychologists to figure out what that will do to a kid's psyche. I will say that I have seen the same dynamic played out, thankfully to a less dramatic degree, in other families over the years. The parent I watched chew out their kid due to some perceived infraction—they didn't hustle, lost focus, or lost to someone they shouldn't have—is the same one calling me to complain about some minor wrong done to their kid that needs correction—another kid cheated, they didn't get to play the right people in clinic, the tournament didn't seed the kid properly, and so on.

This type of overinvolved, obsessive parent has what I would call an aggressively proactive approach to sports parenting. Sometimes kids brought up in this environment do quite well for short periods of time. Their parents make sure their kids are provided with the best coaching, required to practice long hours, play a lot of tournaments, and have the best equipment. But only the most resilient kids can deal with such an intense environment for long. Even those who do make it (which may mean, for example, playing college tennis) have strained relationships with their parents and carry a lot of emotional baggage. At worst they quit, and at best they underachieve.

Of course, most parents are neither 100 percent proactive nor 100 percent reactive. A good illustration would be the case of Kevin, the dad of a nationally ranked junior I was coaching at a prestigious national tournament. I had been coaching his son Christopher for two or three years and had, up to that point, few interactions with Kevin. He didn't seem overly involved in the details but was supportive and content to provide the opportunity for his son to pursue a sport he enjoyed. Kevin had traveled to the tournament along with the parents of two other boys (Christopher's friends) I was coaching. The night before the matches were scheduled to start, I had dinner with the three young men and their parents. The boys were keyed up to play the next day. As a coach, I felt the best thing for the boys was to eat a good dinner, enjoy the evening with their friends and family, and not talk about tennis too much. I needed to keep them focused but relaxed. The challenge was to find ways to guide the conversation away from tennis at a table populated by parents who themselves were anxious about the matches scheduled the next day. Somewhere between ordering and when the food arrived, Kevin commented that he didn't feel I was working the boys hard enough during their practice session that afternoon. Also, he felt that the mood at the dinner table needed to be more serious in light of the importance of the tournament the next day. I disagreed. There was an uncomfortable few minutes of verbal sparring between us as I tried to redirect the conversation. Needless to say, the mood of the evening had changed significantly. Back at the hotel, Kevin apologized for making such a fuss at dinner. But he made it clear that he still felt the same way. As I mentioned earlier, Kevin had been a supportive but fairly uninvolved dad up to this point. All the sudden he had become one of the most proactive parents I had ever dealt with and wanted to take over my role as coach. In his defense, this was the first national tournament he had ever attended. As I well knew, that can do some crazy things to your psyche, whether you're a parent, coach, or player.

This is a great example of the dilemma of sports parenting. If you lean too much toward the reactive style, you risk errors of omission and miss things that are important. If you lean too much toward the proactive style, you risk errors of commission and tend to do things you later regret. It's easy to bounce from one extreme to the other based on emotions, which, in turn, makes for a pretty tough environment for kids (and coaches).

What Now?

So understanding all this, where should you start if you want to have a chance for success as a sports parent?

First, *realize that your natural inclinations may conflict with the best interests of your kid*, and recognize what kind of parenting style you tend towards. Learn to build on your strengths and minimize your weaknesses. It's no different than the approach we coaches take in training your kids.

Second, *understand that individuality and variation are inherent parts of sports parenting* (and coaching). Kids are like snowflakes—they may look the same in a group, but each one is unique. Also, the circumstances in which kids live their lives constantly change. As a result, there can never be a one formula that guarantees success for every kid . . . or even for one kid in every circumstance.

Third, *ask the right questions*. Just after the arrival of our first daughter, I had a conversation with my dad. I was a twenty-seven-year-old tennis pro who had been married for fifteen months with no clear direction in life and a lot of questions. What kind of father would I be? How would we pay for college? How do you change a diaper? And on and on. After a while, he stopped me mid-sentence and said, "You're going to be fine." I asked him to elaborate, thinking that he clearly hadn't been listening. He said that he knew I would be fine because I was asking all the right questions; the answers would come as I went. Some examples of the right questions sports parents have asked me over the years are listed at the beginning of these chapters.

Lastly, *learn principles that lead you down the right path*, and apply them as you deal with the individuality of your kid and the variation in the environment. Years ago I read a business book called *Good to Great*, by Jim Collins. He described an approach that successful business people use to guide their thinking. It is to ask three questions: 1.) Do I have a passion for this? 2.) Can I be really good at it? 3.) Will it make money?

This approach has been invaluable to me in running a business. Planning and decision-making usually fall into place if you are guided by the right principles. In this sense, running a business and sports parenting are no different. They are both about dealing with individuality, change, and challenge. The key to dealing with these is finding the right principles to guide your thoughts and decisions.

Chapter 2

How Do I Coach My Kid?

(Plans vs. Principles)

"Flexibility is the key to stability."

—John Wooden

Team Leaders

In Nick Saviano's excellent book, *Maximum Tennis*, he introduces the helpful concept of *developmental team leader*.[1] Most high-level professional tennis players had a team leader who took the lead role in guiding their athletic development. In many cases, that person was a parent or close relative rather than a coach. The focus of the team

---

[1] For more on this concept, see Nick Saviano, *Maximum Tennis: 10 Keys to Unleashing Your On-Court Potential* (Champaign, IL: Human Kinetics, 2002).

leader is the big picture—logistics, organization, planning, and communication. They also need to understand how the coach fits in with the long-term goals of the player. The coach is someone the team leader decides is best suited for training the player at various stages. So unless you are coaching your own kid, step one in successful sports parenting is to think of yourself more as a team leader than a coach. Keep in mind that the coach's responsibility is paying attention to the details of training. Defining everyone's roles is quite important, because when the lines between the two get blurry—which happens often—problems arise.

I was thinking of this as I sat down to lunch with the dad of one of my students. He wanted to discuss his daughter's tennis and how he might best support her development. I suggested we categorize topics into three groups. First were what I'd call the "ground-level topics": recent matches, stroke production, tactics, and so on. All these were relevant but not, I proposed, most productive for our discussion, since they were best handled by me and his daughter. Second were the "ten-thousand-foot topics": tournament scheduling, training schedules, academics/athletics balance, and parent-coach communication. These were better areas for discussion, because they involved areas in which he should have an active role or at least be aware of. Lastly, were the "thirty-thousand-foot topics": character development, building life skills, and maintaining quality relationships (particularly between him and his daughter). These were the areas that mattered most.

I suggested we first get above the clouds at thirty thousand feet and only after that discuss the topics at the lower levels. That *first* conversation provides an excellent context for the ones that follow. He acknowledged that this made sense but mentioned he still had a lot of concerns relating to ground-level topics. I realized the first thing he needed was an update on what I was working on with his daughter so that he knew those topics were being addressed. As I did this, I sensed he relaxed a bit. I made a mental note to fill him in more often. Second, I suggested that he email me with his thoughts after his daughter played tournaments rather than sharing them with his daughter (which had not been terribly well received by her in the past). That would enable him to get it out of his system without his daughter tuning him out. Lastly, I suggested that his guiding principle when deciding to speak to her on the subject of tennis should be: 1.) when he is asked a question by his daughter, or 2.) when he sees imminent danger to his daughter's physical or emotional well-being.

These are what I call "the Kristin rules" which I implemented at the request of my daughter, Kristin, when she was learning to drive. Apparently, I was spending a little too much time on the ground-level topics. I may have been a tad too verbal as I crammed everything I had ever learned about driving into each outing with Kristin. This was making an already stressful experience even more so. I think there's a clear analogy here. In both cases, well-meaning parents tend to talk too much. The Kristin rules made it more likely that she would listen when I had something important to say. It created a better learning environment and a less stressful experience for both of us.

It's easier to keep the ground-level topics in perspective when you're focused mainly on the thirty-thousand-foot goals. This is what business guru Stephen Covey, in his bestselling book *The Seven Habits of Highly Effective People*, calls beginning with the end in mind. I think this is a great idea for sports parents, because if you know where you want to go, it's a lot easier to chart a course to get there. This means you'll spend more time thinking about what your kid will become through sports than what they achieve in sports. There are two thirty-thousand-foot goals that matter most: first, for your kid to *develop independence*, self-confidence, self-reliance, and self-motivation; and second, to foster an environment that encourages your kid to *love the process* rather than obsess about the outcomes.

Developing Independence

There are a number of things you, as a sports parent, can do to develop independence in your kid. Most of them are best illustrated by my experience with a wire fox terrier named Murphy.

PLANS VS. PRINCIPLES

We got Murphy when he was about eight weeks old, but unfortunately, I didn't begin with the end in mind when he was a puppy. I spent more time playing with him than I did thinking about how he would grow up. As a result, we ended up with a rambunctious dog that required constant attention. About ten years later, I started watching the television series *The Dog Whisperer with Cesar Milan*. Cesar explained a few key principles that helped me. First, good trainers understand that dogs respond best to positive reinforcement. Second, dogs need a pack leader whom they respect and trust. And, most importantly, trainers need to project calm, assertive energy. Since I was lacking in all these areas, I had inadvertently trained my dog in ways bound to produce results inconsistent with my big picture goals, which was to have an obedient, well trained, semi-member of our family that behaved well without constant supervision. I exemplified a management technique that author Kenneth Blanchard calls "leave alone—zap."[2] from *The One Minute Manager meets the Monkey*. I rarely, if ever, gave Murphy positive reinforcement for good behavior, but whenever he did something wrong, I disciplined him big time. I would chase him around the house. My voice would be loud and aggressive, using lots of words I'm certain Murphy didn't understand. And I would occasionally hit him on the butt when I finally caught him, like I was spanking a disobedient child. What dog in his right mind would ever voluntarily listen to an owner like that? Fortunately, once I learned and started implementing Cesar Milan's techniques, Murphy's behavior gradually improved (better late than never). As Cesar often said, dog training is more about training people than about training dogs.

There are lots of applications here for sports parents who would like to develop independent, well-behaved kids through sports. Starting with Cesar's main three principles: use positive reinforcement, be a leader who earns respect, and project calm, assertive energy. Here are the main lessons I learned as I applied those principles and how they relate to sports parenting.

---

[2] See Ken Blanchard, *The One Minute Manager Meets the Monkey, audio CD disc 2* (New York: Simon and Schuster audio division, 1988).

First, success in any sport, particularly an individual sport like tennis, requires problem-solving skills, self-reliance, and personal responsibility. These are all things that kids have to learn on their own time. But parents, coaches, and teachers can help create the right conditions for that to happen. If I had identified my end goals when Murphy was a puppy, and acted accordingly, I wouldn't have had to spend so much time and effort retraining him once he was grown.

Second, remember that it's not about your intentions (which are usually good); it is about how your kid is internalizing what you are doing (this might not always be good). The gap between those two can often be huge. My intentions were good with Murphy. I loved that dog and wanted him to learn to behave well. However, I didn't have a clue about training a dog properly, so he never internalized good habits of behavior. My focus on discipline instead of positive reinforcement led to an unintended result. Murphy only behaved well if it was forced upon him, not because he was trained well.

Third, kids get conditioned to whatever you, as a sports parent, do consistently and often. If you are constantly evaluating and criticizing your kid, sooner or later they will become overly self-critical, not to mention dependent on you for constant affirmation. My intention in disciplining Murphy, with lots of talking and an occasional pop on the butt, was meant to get him to behave well. But all that did was to condition him to run in the opposite direction. Relative to sports parenting, this means that if you want your kid to be independent, sometimes it's best to calm down and talk less. This doesn't mean you can't express an opinion or impose consequences occasionally. But like any good coach, your job is mostly to observe. Speak when you have something positive and constructive to say. The goal is to get them to associate your involvement in a positive way. This is what I think Cesar meant by calm, assertive energy.

Fourth, in order to develop independent, well-behaved kids, you have to expect, and allow for, some failure. This, of course, takes lots of discipline and patience. It's a process that takes time. This can be challenging for parents who want quick results and see their role more as a fixer than facilitator. Training allows for some degree of failure; enablement allows for none. There's a big difference. Kids learn best to solve problems, take responsibility, and develop confidence when they're given the freedom to fail. Without the risk of failure, the successes don't mean much anyway.

Kids raised by parents who understand and implement these lessons learn independence and gain a sense of accomplishment that's addictive and habit forming. They learn to see challenges as opportunities, and they develop a confidence that has implications in life well beyond sports.

Risking Freedom

When you watch great athletes in the heat of competition you rarely see them smile, but you always get the sense that there's no place they'd rather be. They have a sense of purpose that goes beyond the superficial. No kid stays engaged in sports long-term without developing this type of passion for their sport. That doesn't mean they are always happy. It does mean they find satisfaction in overcoming the challenges that are an inevitable part of pursuing anything worthwhile. No matter how great the win, the high will fade. The question will always be: What next? Joy is found in the pursuit of that next challenge, in the process rather than the achievement. The key thing to remember is that, as a parent or coach, we aren't responsible for providing joy. We can't make them have a passion for the sport. That can only come from them. Your job, as a parent, is to focus on providing an environment that increases the likelihood that your kid will develop a love of the game. Trying to force the issue is not only futile but usually detrimental.

This was illustrated in a workout I did with two teenage boys, Scott and Matt, a few years ago. Scott's parents were avid players and quite involved in Scott's tennis. They clearly wanted their son to have a passion for the sport. Scott and I both knew that if Scott chose not to pursue tennis, his parents would be quite disappointed. Matt's parents, in contrast, were supportive but not overly involved. I knew that if Matt had chosen not to pursue tennis, they would genuinely be OK with that. Both sets of parents had good intentions, but they sent very different messages to their kids. Scott carried the weight of his parent's expectations and overinvolvement; Matt didn't have to carry that burden. Scott saw challenges as obstacles; Matt saw them as opportunities.

Scott was the more talented player. He had effortless power and flowed around the court. Physically, things came fairly easy to him. Mentally, though, he rarely seemed to enjoy competing. Matt, on the other hand, had to work for every ball he made. His strengths were his intensity, competitiveness, and work ethic.

One day I scheduled the boys to train together and had them play a series of games to 11. Scott started off well, winning most of the points easily. Matt looked frustrated but determined. Somewhere around the middle of the first game, things started to change. Scott missed a few shots, which unnerved him. He barely won the first game as his level of play started to drop. During the last few points, he looked as if he wasn't trying all that hard.

I could sense the workout was headed downhill, so I brought the boys in for a quick talk. I encouraged them both to stay engaged, mentally and physically, regardless of outcome. I knew Matt was prone to trying too hard when challenged. Scott was more likely to stop trying altogether when things got tough. Either way, I knew the quality level of that practice session was at risk. The only points Scott was winning were those in which his talent made it easy, quick points where he would go for a powerful, risky shot and hit a winner.[3] Matt continued to play with determination regardless of how many winners Scott hit. The next few games all ended in Matt's favor with increasingly lopsided scores. It was clear that Scott, while he may have enjoyed hitting winners, had no desire to work without the assurance he would get rewarded by winning easily. Matt was willing to compete regardless of outcome, adversity, or frustration; he found joy in the battle.

Author Angela Duckworth has recently brought attention to the concept of *grit*, in an excellent book of that title.[4] The word is hard to define but even harder to develop. Whatever the exact definition, it was clear that on a tennis court, Matt had it and Scott didn't. No pep talk from me was going to change that. Scott simply didn't have passion for the sport, so he wasn't wired to deal with much adversity. This was partially due to his temperament but also to his parent's expectations and involvement. Ironically, a parent who cares most about their kid's developing passion for a sport often creates an environment less likely to produce that result. Parents who give kids freedom to find their own

---

[3] For non-tennis folks, a winner is a powerful or sharply-angled shot that bounces twice before the opponent can get their racquet on it.

[4] See Angela Duckworth, *Grit: The Power of Passion and Perseverance* (New York: Scribner, 2016). I also recommend Duckworth's very popular TED talk on the topic, which is easily available on YouTube.

passion, take the risk that their kids won't choose that sport. But their kids are more likely to succeed if and when they do. Scott's parents didn't want to take the risk; Matt's parents did. As a result, Matt developed a passion for the sport that was genuine. That had a far greater impact on the disparity between Scott and Matt than their skill levels.

What's the Plan?

If you accept the premise that the goal of sports parenting should be to develop independent kids who are passionate about their sport, the logical question becomes: How do I do that? Or, in other words, what's the plan? That's a question I've been asked many times. Unfortunately, the answer is not simple.

Years ago I had a conversation with Michael, the dad of a promising junior in our program named Jason. Michael was an engineer by vocation, and since I was raised by an engineer myself, I had a pretty good idea of how he thought. He was a no-nonsense, clear-thinking guy who liked to gather information, come up with a plan, and execute the plan. Michael called me one day to discuss Jason's future. He was concerned that Jason wasn't improving quickly enough, and he asked if I could provide a plan that would ensure that Jason would "move to the next level." That's a term commonly used by tennis parents who usually mean they want their kid to beat other kids perceived to be better than their own. He also mentioned that he would like Jason to earn a college scholarship. The first thing I explained to Michael was that developing kids in sports wasn't analogous to designing a building. There wasn't any one plan we could design that would guarantee long-term success. His son had developed into a fine player, not because of some grand plan that he or I (as Jason's coach) had laid out years ago. He was doing well because he loved to play a game and, thanks to his dad, had been fortunate enough to be provided the environment in which he could pursue it. Jason had detailed coaching that focused on making sure he had the right fundamentals (technical, mental, and strategic). He was playing all the right tournaments, was a hard worker, and had plenty of opportunities for practicing with other players at, or above, his level. Continuing along that path would offer the best chances for success. But, I explained, none of it *ensured* a specific result.

I mentioned to Michael that plans, programs, and goals all had a useful purpose, but there were too many variables involved to guarantee outcomes. The best we could do would be to increase the odds. For many parents, a plan implies that a specific result will happen in a given time frame. They often look to the coach to provide the plan and their kid to execute it. The problem is that sports, and people, just don't work like that. You never know what's going to happen, regardless of how great the plan is.

As I write this, I have recently enjoyed watching the NCAA basketball tournament, and it's clear to me that basketball offers excellent examples of this concept. Every team's coach starts with a game plan but knows full well that the plan doesn't ensure victory. That doesn't mean you don't make one or that you don't try to carry it out; it just means you don't go in expecting things to work out exactly like you planned. One main reason for this, of course, is that the other team has a plan designed with a goal that is precisely the opposite of yours: beating your team. This is why when you hear coaches talk about their plans for the game, they talk some about the specifics but mostly emphasize the principles they have tried to instill in their players—teamwork, hustle, toughness, and so on. This has a lot more to do with winning than designing the perfect game plan.

My academic career was average at best, because I didn't spend a lot of time trying to understand the concepts behind what I was studying. Memorizing enough to get by on the next test got me through. Looking back, I regret not making the effort to understand the principles. I've known a lot of sports parents who have felt the same way after their kids have grown up. They understand, in hindsight, that they were focused on short-term results and the plans to achieve them but spent little time thinking about the principles that would lead to results in the long term. If you try to come up with a plan at each stage without some overarching principles that provide context, you generally make things a lot harder than they need to be. Knowing the right principles usually leads to the right plan as a by-product. Understanding this is invaluable because it helps keep things in perspective when things aren't going well. Every small blip on the radar screen doesn't mean that it's time for a new plan. I know that may sound like bad news to some parents, and it didn't go over terribly well with Jason's dad that day. But it's the truth.

The right question isn't "What's the plan?" It's "What are the principles that lead to the plan?" Plans may change, but principles stay the same. One key principle is that, as a sports parent, you are a team leader whose responsibility is to provide an encouraging, supportive environment in which your kid can develop independence through and passion for their sport. It's more about providing an environment for success than a plan that guarantees it.

Chapter 3

How Do We Choose the Right Coach and Program?

(Form vs. Substance)

"Truly great teachers and coaches have a . . . Zen-like blend of focus and calm developed by people who have to spend inordinate amounts of time sitting in one place watching closely while someone else does something."

—David Foster Wallace

Coaching Moments

The default measurement people have of any junior program—academic or athletic—always seems to center around who the top achievers are. The first question I usually got asked by parents about our tennis academy was, "Do you have any good kids in the program?" I always wanted to ask them in response, "Good relative to whom?" Most of the time, I just said yes and moved on.

I think a far better question is, "Do you have a challenging, engaging environment?" More specifically, "Do you have a program that consistently pushes players outside their comfort zones?" To me, the measurement of a junior program should be about how many coaching moments, how many opportunities for kids to develop technically, strategically, and mentally, it provides.

One of the best illustrations of this is when kids compete on a ladder system. In this system, players who win move up and those less fortunate move down.[1] Since they compete based on results, mismatches in age, size, gender, ranking, or reputation sometimes occur. This forces kids to be accountable, to respect every opponent, and to compete against a variety of game styles. It's occasionally humbling, often uncomfortable, and certainly challenging.

In one case, Megan (age sixteen) had just rotated down to play Jacob (age eleven). I could tell Megan was disappointed that she'd moved down and had to play a younger kid. She had everything to lose and nothing to gain. Jacob seemed excited to play an older kid but also somewhat

---

[1] "Those less fortunate," a phrase I picked up from my friend David Johnson, is a bit more protective of self-esteem than *loser*. I still use it occasionally, although I sometimes get strange looks from the kids.

intimidated, worried about losing badly before they even started playing. The up-side was that he was playing with house money—nothing to lose, everything to gain. As they started to play, it was obvious Megan was uptight; she was pressing just a bit too much and easily frustrated. Jacob, on the other hand, was fully engaged, enjoying playing a better player and rising to the challenge. As they got near the end of a game to 15, the score was 14-13 in Megan's favor. I felt like I was watching the finals of a tournament. Jacob was staying focused even after Megan would overpower him with an occasional winner, and Megan was staying under control mentally even after the occasional error. She was being forced to deal with one of the hardest challenges any tennis player faces: being the favored player against an underdog who is playing well.

To the credit of both of them, they each played beautifully. Jacob was stroking through the ball and staying consistent; Megan was doing the same, courageously trying to maneuver her opponent around the court. Finally, after a long rally, Megan got an opening and hit a winner as Jacob hustled over, vainly reaching out for it at full speed. I could feel Megan's relief and Jacob's frustration. From many years of watching competitive kids like these, I knew the only thing in either of their minds was the outcome. Megan, was happy (and relieved) that she won. Jacob was frustrated (and disappointed) that he lost.

I sensed the opportunity for a coaching moment, so I brought them up to the net and explained that they had pushed each other way outside one another's comfort zones and, as result, had gotten great practice regardless of the outcome. Although I've learned that in coaching you never really know what sticks in people's minds, both kids seemed to understand. Hopefully, the key lesson learned was that there is more going on in practice than simply winning (moving up) or losing (moving down). Regardless of the result, if they could learn to consistently practice at that level of intensity, they would build competitive skills that few players attain. Ironically, I knew that they were less likely to do that in the next round because they would be playing familiar opponents. Great practice rarely happens unless you are uncomfortable mentally, physically, and/or emotionally. Comfort is the enemy of progress.[2]

These concepts, by the way, are contrary to the prevailing school of thought when it comes to junior development. This school is based on the assumption that the best way to improve is to practice with players who are better than you. Tennis players, and many of their parents, who ascribe to this type of thinking focus primarily on other players. Which brings us back to the often-asked question, "Do you have any good players in the program?" But great practice

---

[2] This is a saying we used constantly in our program. I credit my friend and longtime colleague Chris Hoshour for his wisdom here.

has little to do with other people. It has everything to do with a player's own ability to play to a high standard regardless of the opponent, circumstance, or situation.

So, if you are a parent looking for a place for your kid to train, look for one that's more program-based than player-based, one that's focused on consistently creating an organized, engaging, challenging environment rather than one focused on ensuring your kid always gets to play with the highest-level or most promising kids. Remember also that the most valuable learning often happens in unlikely circumstances, against a variety of opponents, and usually when you aren't watching.

Psychological Contracts: Pros or Coaches?

My friend Drew, who, like me, spends much of his professional life coaching junior tennis players, called me a few years ago to discuss an issue that we both dealt with often. He had just returned from a weekend tournament that he'd attended to watch some of his students play. Drew didn't charge for this service, preferring to have the flexibility to go wherever he'd be most useful (tournaments often have multiple sites). When he got back, he got a call from one of his students' moms. She was unsatisfied with the amount of time Drew had spent watching her kid at the tournament. Through the grapevine she had somehow determined that he had spent more time with other students and was upset her kid didn't get equal time. Drew mentioned how frustrating it was not to be appreciated for the time and effort he had made. He wondered why he should make the effort to go to tournaments in the future since the only feedback he got was that complaint. I reminded him to keep things in perspective and not make any hasty decisions; this was just one selfish parent with unrealistic expectations (this is a mantra you have to repeat to yourself occasionally when you work with junior tennis parents).

Around this time, my daughter Kara was studying elementary education in college. She introduced me to a term she had learned at school: *psychological contract*. The academic world uses it to refer to the unspoken expectations parents have of their children's teachers. The problem is that those expectations vary from parent to parent, are never clearly spelled out, and can be unrealistic. This, of course, can lead to real problems for everyone—parents, teachers, and kids. This reminded me of my discussion with Drew. Clearly that self-centered mom had expected more from Drew at the tournament. She had an unspoken, but very real, psychological contract with him and clearly felt he had not lived up to his part of the deal.

As Drew and I continued our conversation, I thought about how we use the terms *tennis pro* and *tennis coach* interchangeably—and how easily this can lead to problems. Here's how I would define each and the difference between the two.

A *tennis pro* is someone who gets paid hourly to provide instruction on technique, strategy, emotional control, and physical skills or to give general advice on any topic that impacts tennis performance. The player should expect the pro's full attention for the time allotted. It is also reasonable to expect some time off-court to be spent scheduling, giving feedback on progress, or advice on tournaments, although none of this off-court time is paid time for the pro. Even though many pros occasionally travel to tournaments to watch students play, this should not be expected but appreciated.

A *tennis coach* is someone who provides all the services of the tennis pro but who also spends significant amounts of time off-court supporting, advising, and counseling players and parents. It's reasonable to expect a coach to travel to tournaments to watch players compete, but they should be compensated accordingly. High school coaches, for example, get paid a salary to coach a team. Coaches of pro players also get salaries and often a percentage of the player's prize money.

This can all get muddled pretty easily, since many pros function as coaches at tournaments. That tends to heighten the expectations of parents, which is what caused the problem in Drew's situation.

The point here is that it would be helpful to explain the distinction between a pro and coach as a first step in communication between pros, players, and parents. That way, the roles are defined and everyone has realistic expectations. When Drew and I concluded our discussion, we settled on the following analogy as a way of thinking about this topic. Hiring a tennis pro is like ordering à la carte from the menu at a restaurant. You pick what you want and pay for what specifically suits your needs. Hiring a tennis coach is like eating at the buffet. You can choose from a variety of foods, go back as much as you want, and pay just one price. Problems occur when the parents or players think they are eating at the buffet when they are paying à la carte—which, we concluded, was the assumption that mom had made that weekend. As in any relationship, the key to success is communicating well. Defining the difference between a tennis pro and tennis coach would have been a great place to start in this case.

What to Look For

I've always been interested, from a business standpoint, in why parents choose one junior program or coach over another. Most of our business was built through referrals, and I had hoped that parents recommended our program because of the quality of our coaching and professionalism. I think the reality is that many parents sent their kids to us simply because of other kids who were already in the program—their kid had a friend in the program, they heard we had other good kids to practice with, and so on. These aren't bad reasons, but, as I often point out, thinking about other people too much can lead to problems. The players in any program represent only the form, (how things look from the outside) not the substance (what happens on the inside). And the substance of any program is dictated by the coaches who are running the show. If you accept that premise, then your next question might be, "How do I know if the coaching is good?" What follows are a few thoughts on what qualities to look for:

Google coaches

I read an article a few years ago about Larry Page and Sergey Brin, the guys who founded Google, that mentioned a unique principle they used to build the company: Focus first on the users (the public), who pay nothing, and second on the customers (the advertisers), who provide the revenue. This was counter to conventional business theory, but it sure has worked at Google. I realized that, right or wrong, this is how I've thought about the business of junior tennis for many years. The kids are the users, the parents are the customers. Even though the parents provide the revenue, I've always made the kids my first priority. For some parents, especially those who are really into tennis, this can be hard to accept. This is not to say that a parent shouldn't expect their kid's coach to be accessible for feedback, advice, and so on. I'm sure Google doesn't ignore their advertisers; it's just that they are more passionate about providing a good experience for their users. This is a good quality to look for in tennis pros as well.

Bottom line for parents: Look for a coach who's more passionate about coaching your kid than catering to you.

Billie Jean King coaches

Years ago, when I was first starting to get into coaching junior tennis, the American tennis great Billie Jean King was in town. I heard her mention in an interview that an essential quality for a good coach is that they should always be ready to get fired. That was a new concept to me. I thought of how often I worried about what the parents of our students were thinking. Were they unhappy with who their kid was playing in clinic? Was I always direct and open about what I thought could help the student, or was I more concerned about the reaction of the parent or player? Would this cause conflict and perhaps cause them to go elsewhere?

In a culture of consumerism and competition, people have choices, and some parents will take their kids somewhere else when they don't hear what they like. Because of this, it's easy, as a coach, to operate from a fearful mindset. This can lead to caring more about pleasing parents rather than doing what's right for kids. Coaching junior sports can be a test of integrity that takes a lot more courage than people realize. I think that's exactly what Billie Jean was talking about when she said you can't be an effective coach unless you are willing to get fired every day.

Bottom line for parents: Look for a coach who is direct, honest, and willing to tell you what you need to hear rather than only what you want to hear.

Delivery room coaches

When my wife was in the hospital waiting to deliver our second daughter, she was attached to a fetal monitor to keep track of the baby's heartbeat. I had seen this before due to my wealth of experience; after all, this was our second child. As we waited and talked, I noticed the baby's heartbeat on the screen was gone. Naturally, I panicked and went running into the hall to alert what I hoped would be a team of doctors. A nurse appeared and calmly explained that when the mom shifts, the monitor can lose the signal. Not a big deal—she had seen this occur countless times before and easily adjusted the monitor.[3] Thankfully, she had a better perspective based on her years of experience.

I've thought back on this often as I've dealt with the parents of young tennis players. They often see a situation that seems urgent (but really isn't) and treat it like I did, doing the equivalent of running into the hall and yelling for the

---

[3] In case you were wondering, our daughter was born with no complications that day healthy and happy - despite her dad's histrionics.

nurse. Stressing out over your kid having to play the #1 seed in a tournament, being upset they lost a close match, or losing after having a lead all fall into this category. It's easy to become overly emotional when you care a lot but have limited experience, knowledge, or perspective. To gain the experience and knowledge of the nurse (or a tennis pro), you have to become one.

Bottom line for parents: Look for a coach who is calm under pressure and trust their judgment. Emotion on your part should not equate to an emergency on their part.

Call-you-back coaches

When I first started Charlotte Tennis Academy, the office's telephone answering machine was an essential tool in communicating with our clients. Since I was on the court most of the time, the first thing I did when I returned to the office was call people back. On many occasions, I was amazed at the response I got. People would thank me profusely for getting back to them so quickly. They would tell me about the tennis pro or plumber or contractor who never called them back. I thought to myself, "If this is all I have to do to set myself apart from the competition, then our business should be very successful." However, I noticed that this got harder as time went on. There were many nights when I was tired and just wanted to go home to shower, eat, and see my family. I learned that professionalism comes down to paying attention to details, and that often takes more time, effort, and discipline than you realize at first.

Bottom line for parents: Look for a coach who gets back to you promptly when you call, text, or email. If they are professional enough to do that, they are most likely coaching your kid with the same attention to detail.

Tennis Pros and Car Mechanics

One of the most important responsibilities parents have as team leaders is choosing a coach. Team leaders are crucial in overseeing the big picture, but coaches have a tremendous impact on the specifics at each stage of development. Finding a good coach can be a challenging task. As in any field, there are people who are the real deal and those who just look the part. It's often hard to tell one from the other.

I thought of this a few years ago when I attended the funeral of Johnny Parker, the owner of Compact Car Service here in Charlotte. Johnny, as everyone in our family came to know him, was our go-to guy when it came to servicing our cars. We had often felt taken advantage of when dealing with car repair people—extra fees, hidden problems, and so on. All these guys, and their shops, looked the same to us (as did the undersides of our cars). When we discovered Johnny's shop, things were different. He seemed to care about us and was passionate about his job. There were never any surprises, and when Johnny explained something we could usually understand what he was talking about. Over the many years we took our cars to his shop, we found Johnny to be competent, professional, and trustworthy. In our experience, this was a rare combination for people in his line of work.

The last time I stood side by side with Johnny was when he invited my daughter Kara and me into the shop to look over a used car she was considering buying. I had gone through a similar process numerous times with cars I had bought over the years. Each time Johnny saved me from buying a clunker because his standards were so high. I knew that if he said a car was in good shape, then it was worth making an offer. This was the fourth car Kara had brought to him. True to form, he had rejected the previous three for various reasons. As we stood with him around the car, he did all the things he had done with the cars I had brought him in years past—pointed out issues I would never have noticed, prioritized the repairs needed in order of importance, and provided the estimates for the work. By the way, as regular customers Johnny never charged us for this service - impressive.

As Kara and I left to return to the dealership, we compared notes on Johnny's master class; he could pack a lot of information into ten minutes. After all those years, Johnny truly felt like family. Kara had grown up with my wife and me talking about him. Now she was shopping for her first car with Johnny as her advisor, and it felt like a rite of passage into adulthood for her. He liked this particular car (and so did Kara), so she used the information Johnny had provided to negotiate and bought it.

I share this story, first, because it feels good to share Johnny's memory with others. He was an inspiration for me, and I think of him often. Second, because it illustrates the fact that we never know, when we meet people, who has character and substance until we deal with them for a while. One tennis pro looks pretty much like the next, and they often speak a language people find hard to understand, just like car mechanics. It's pretty easy to dazzle people with bullshit—a line Johnny would use from time to time. In my field of junior tennis, savvy pros figure out what people want to hear pretty quickly. If we want to dazzle, all we have to do is wait for an opportunity to drop the names of highly ranked kids in our program, mention some kids we've coached who have received college scholarships, and maybe even throw in stories about our own accomplishments as players. However, usually the people who do the most talking are the ones with the least ability to get the job done—form over substance. Over time, the cream rises to the top, as they say. The only way to know that a tennis pro (or program) has substance is to get to know them for some reasonable length of time, say four to six weeks. When you see the qualities I found in Johnny (character, competence, consistency, and caring), you will have found the right coach.

Chapter 4

How Do "We" Get to the Next Level?

(Outcome vs. Process)

*"If you focus on results, you will never change.
If you focus on change, you will always get results."*

—Sign at my doctor's office

Practicing with Intensity

When I first moved to Charlotte, an acquaintance asked if I would play a few practice sets with a fourteen-year-old, nationally-ranked junior named Peter Ayers. I was in my late twenties, a veteran of four years of Division 1 college tennis and two years of professional tennis, and I was playing the best tennis of my life. I agreed to meet Peter at a local club but didn't have high expectations for getting much practice.

Although I won the first two sets quickly, Peter made sure I had to work for it. I was surprised at what good practice it was; for a fourteen-year-old kid, he really hit the ball well. We had lots of good points, even if Peter was on the losing end of most of them. The guys I usually practiced with would have called it a day. Peter, however, wanted to keep going. I still have a mental picture of looking over the net to serve as we began the third set. He looked focused, ready to compete, and was clearly unaffected by the poor outcomes of the previous sets. His only concern seemed to be getting the most out of the opportunity to practice with me. I think I won that third set pretty easily, but what I've never forgotten was Peter's competitiveness during that practice session. I can count on one hand the number of players I've known who practiced with that level of intensity. They were all Division 1 college players or professionals—never fourteen-year-old kids.

Our paths rarely crossed over the next two years, since Peter was playing a lot of tournaments and I was busy teaching tennis. Due to his practice habits, I knew that he was probably improving quickly. I found out just how much he improved when we met in a tournament when he was sixteen years old. He beat me 7-6 in the third set. Not long after that, he was recruited to play college tennis at Duke, where he went on to have an outstanding college career. None of this was surprising to me, although I didn't particularly enjoy getting beat by a sixteen-year-old at that tournament.

Around the same time I met Peter, I had the opportunity to start practicing with Tim Wilkison, a touring pro from Charlotte who needed a sparring partner when he was in town. I remembered watching Tim play on TV at the US Open before I moved to Charlotte. He was known as an overachiever who hustled for every ball, never let up, and played with unrelenting intensity. The first few times we practiced I was nervous and I didn't play very well, but Tim always respected me enough to give his full effort. Everything he did on the practice court looked exactly like it did when he was playing on TV against the best players in the world. We often played on a back court at 6:30 a.m. (which seemed to be Tim's favorite practice time) with not one person watching. He played every point as if it were match point at Wimbledon, even though he was usually beating me handily. I've never met anyone who brought that level of intensity to a practice session. I don't believe that I ever beat him outright; maybe I won a groundstroke game to 11 once in a while. To win points (let alone games) against Tim was extremely demanding, and it was hard for me not to get discouraged. I have a standing rule, though, that if anyone who has been top one hundred in the world asks me to practice I will be there, even at 6:30 a.m., and I'll give it all I've got.

Before training with Tim and Peter, I had always sought out players to practice with who were close to my skill level or slightly better. I thought this was a prerequisite to getting quality practice. But the practices I had with those guys were some of the most productive I've ever had. It was irrelevant that I was a better player (at the time) than Peter or that Tim was a better player than I was. The only things that mattered were that we all pushed ourselves to practice with intensity, kept a positive attitude, and committed to improving regardless of the level of the opponent. This was something I'd never understood before and that I'm grateful to have learned from Peter and Tim. If I had grasped this at an earlier age, I think I would have become a much better player.

When you oversee a junior tennis academy parents have a lot of questions about where their kids will be placed in a group, who else is in the program, and so on. There's no doubt these are legitimate questions but they're challenging because answering them reinforces the same misconception I had: that *who* you're practicing with is more important than how you're practicing. This leads to a mentality that focuses more on outcome than process. Often, I try to use this as an opportunity to pass along the lessons I learned playing with Peter and Tim: *your toughest opponent will always be yourself* (maybe a good line for a t-shirt or a tattoo), so who you're playing doesn't matter all that much. And it's not about whether you're winning right now; it's about trusting that if you keep improving, good results inevitably follow. I've found that it's an uphill battle to sell parents and kids on these concepts. In light of how long it took me to get it, I suppose I understand.

Getting to the Next Level

If the most common question I get from parents is about who the other kids are, the second most common is, "How do we"—meaning parent, coach, and player—"get them to the next level?"

A few things to keep in mind here. First, the "next level" shouldn't be about comparing your kid to another kid; it's about your kid getting better. This is a subtle but important distinction, particularly in an individual sport like tennis. There are too many variables when you deal with other people, and you have no control over how much or how little they're improving. Better to focus on where you are now and how to improve from there: compare yourself to yourself, not to other people. Second, once you achieve the next level, keep in mind there will always be another next level. It's a never-ending process—which, of course, is why coaches are always talking to players about focusing on process (performance) rather than outcomes (comparisons).

Also, be forewarned that getting to the next level in junior tennis, particularly as kids get to higher levels, can be challenging for a variety of reasons. First, the pool of people to practice with and compete against will continually get smaller as players get better. It's a pyramid and, by definition, not everyone can get to the top. Second, tennis players (and more than a few parents) are notorious for being hypercompetitive and self-centered, which means that not everyone gets along. Quite often the players who would most benefit from practicing with each other are the least likely to do so. And third, the pool of good coaches who work with high-level players is limited. There aren't many players at the top of the pyramid, so focusing on the ones that are is not a great business model.

With all this in mind, it's understandable that people call a junior tennis academy to help their kids get to the next level, since they provide access to compatible practice partners through clinics and lessons. Of course, I think that's a good place to start. However, *the best players get the most out of the training they pay for (clinics, lessons) by doing things they don't pay for.* So for the players who are really serious about improving, I offer the following advice:

1. *Create a player development plan* that takes into account all the various factors of your game; establish a vision, set up goals, and create a weekly schedule based on a prioritized list of things you need to work on most. A coach would be helpful at this stage. If you

OUTCOME VS. PROCESS

don't have a coach doing it yourself is OK since you're more likely to stick with a plan you create.[1]

2. *Establish a call list of people* to practice with that includes a wide range of players. Be open to practicing with anyone who is willing to play. Don't buy into the misconception that the only people worth practicing with are better players than you. Plan out how often you want to practice and start making calls. You may be uncomfortable at first doing this. Getting rejected when people say no (or don't show up) can make you feel like a salesman. Stick with it. This is one of the key habits that set players apart from those who only take clinics and lessons.

3. *Learn to practice on your own* when you are unable to schedule someone else to hit with. Self-feeding drills, hitting against a backboard or ball machine, target serving, and fitness/agility workouts are all options. When your ability to train isn't dependent on other people, you open up a wider range of practice options. Even when going to a clinic or lesson, go early or stay late in order to do something from this list.

---

[1] For more on this process, I recommend (again) Saviano's *Maximum Tennis*. Chapter 1 lays out the framework for player development plans.

4. *Learn to play to your standard* regardless of the environment and independent of player, level, age, game style, playing conditions, or the context you're playing in (for example, practice or tournament). The ability to do this requires constant attention, great attitude, tremendous discipline, and unwavering focus. It takes lots of practice and is way harder to do than most players (and parents) realize.

5. *Consider playing more tournaments* as a way of getting more practice matches. This is especially important if you are having trouble finding strong competition or consistent practice partners. Think of tournaments as a way to get good practice on the weekends rather than a way to improve your ranking. It's OK if you're not always in peak condition for every event if you think of tournaments as training opportunities.[2]

---

[2] When I mention this to people I am reminded of a kid I coached named Jennifer (at the time around 13), who had become one of the best players in the country in her age group. She was finding it difficult to find local players at her level to practice with but wasn't interested in moving away to train at an academy. At a tournament we ran into USTA coach Lynn Rolley who told us that she had a student named Lindsay Davenport who had faced a similar challenge when she was a junior. Lynn told us that Lindsay had found it helpful to play more tournaments as a way of getting quality practice without the need to move away from home. Jennifer took that advice to heart and started playing more tournaments—which demonstrated pretty good judgment on her part, considering that Lindsay Davenport (at age 22) would become the no. 1 player in the world at around this same time.

The key to improvement is to do these types of things consistently over a long period of time. Setting yourself apart from the competition is all about doing what others either don't know to do or don't want to do. Do the work, particularly the work that others aren't doing, and the results will follow.

Realistic Encouragement

One reason sports parenting can be a real challenge is that sometimes even the best-intentioned comments can have unintended consequences. An example of this is the case of a thirteen-year-old boy I was coaching who had just won his first tournament. In an effort to be encouraging, his dad told him that due to that win, he should expect success in the next tournament. I didn't think there was anything wrong with that idea, but I warned the dad to be careful with how far he took it. His son could easily interpret that to mean he should do well in every tournament he played, which was unrealistic and would cause him to feel undo pressure.

I told the dad that it was fine to celebrate the win, but it also represented an opportunity to educate his son on the nature of competitive sports. Performance and outcomes vary based on a number of factors—some are in your control, and some aren't. You're never as good as you feel after your best win, but never as bad as you feel after your worst loss. The goal is to minimize the time spent performing poorly and maximize the periods when you perform well; the reality is that you'll be somewhere in the middle most of the time.

Most competitive kids, and many of their parents, have trouble establishing objective standards, because they are rarely satisfied with anything other than above average performance. This is one reason why there's so much dysfunction and burnout in junior sports. By definition, above average can't happen all the time or it wouldn't be above average. Most days you will perform slightly above or below your baseline. This reflects your present, realistic skill level. Players who expect their performance to consistently be above their baseline set themselves up to be frustrated. When you watch them play, they rarely, if ever, seem to be enjoying themselves. When they play above their baseline, they're asking themselves, "Why can't I play like this all the time?" When they play below their baseline, they're asking themselves, "Why am I playing so terrible today?" Players with this mindset are constantly stressed out. This, in turn, leads them to play below their baseline more often. They still improve over time but don't improve as quickly as players who have more reasonable expectations and realistic perspectives. Here are some charts that represent how this looks.

OUTCOME VS. PROCESS

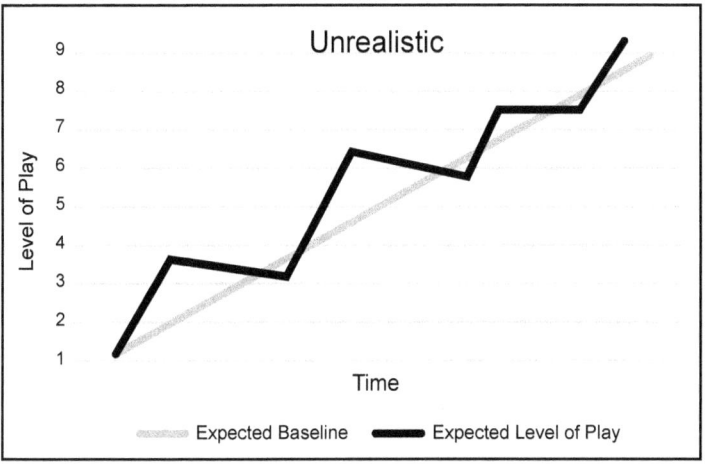

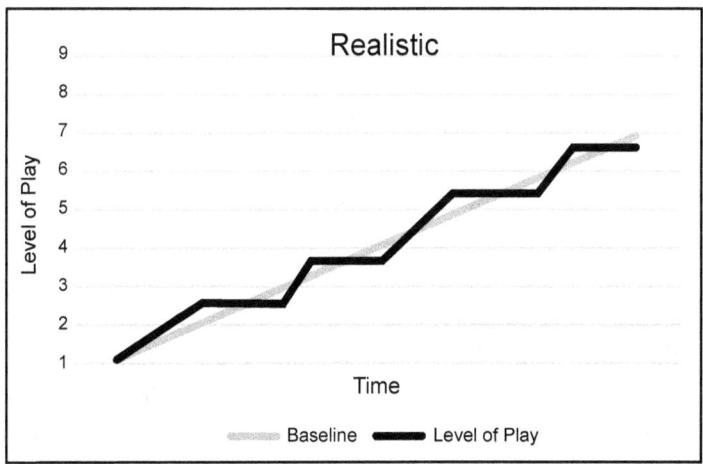

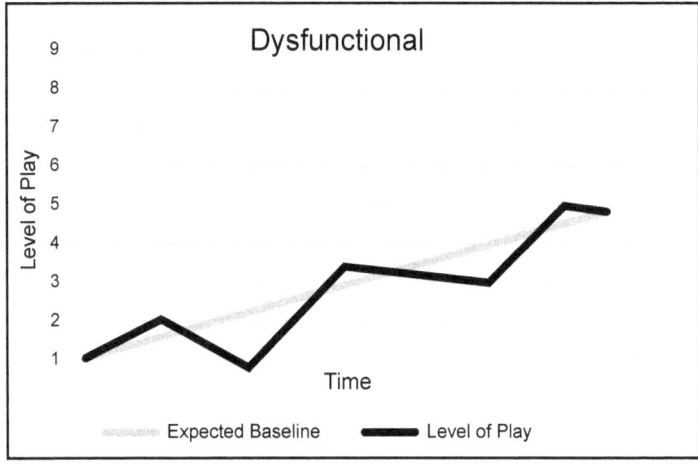

Another thing to keep in mind is that sometimes there are quick spikes in performance, just like growth spurts in thirteen-year-old boys. The key here is not to get overexcited and expect this to last indefinitely. The reality is that at some point, the rate of improvement will plateau for periods of time. This is when a lot of promising kids get discouraged, because they expected to keep improving at a rate that was unsustainable. When they are no longer improving rapidly, the gratification comes less quickly and the sport feels more like work than play. Understanding this concept enables players and parents to set expectations more in line with reality, and to stay the course when improvement levels off. When expectations don't line up with reality, it leads to frustration, and frustrated players have a hard time sustaining high levels of performance over long periods of time.

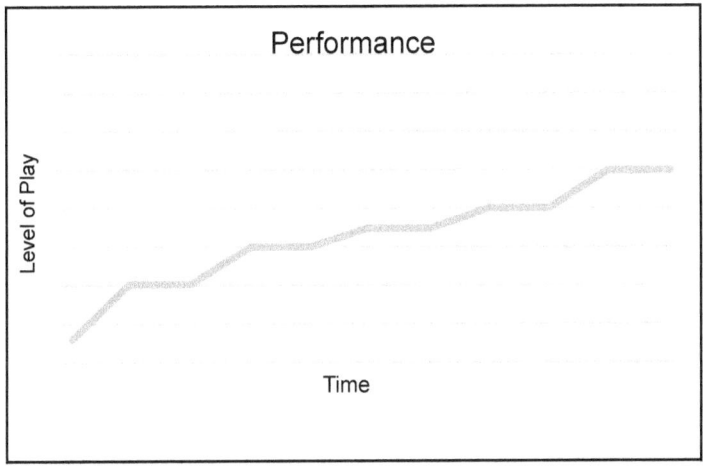

Experienced coaches know that when players are doing well, it's best to focus on areas of improvement rather than dwell on the wins. It's a good time to bring players down a bit so they stay humble and focused. When players are doing poorly, it's best to build them up. This can be counterintuitive if you're a parent who tends to get overexcited when things are going well or overreacts when things are going poorly. In the case of the dad who wanted to encourage his son after his first tournament win, I suggested he stay focused on his son's long-term improvement rather than short-term results (process rather than outcome), regardless of how the next tournament went. This would enable him to be realistically encouraging when things went well while modeling a good perspective when they didn't.

The charts above relate to the timelines for a junior athlete, or someone learning a sport. As I finished writing this section I got to wondering what the timeline might look like over a lifetime. Here are some bullet points describing my personal timeline of skill development (stages 1-4) and inevitable decline (stages 5-6).

- Stage 1 (age 13-17): introduction to tennis, high school tennis, junior tournaments, impact of a great high school coach (thank you, Terry McMahon)
- Stage 2 (age 17-21): exposure to high-level college tennis environment (thank you, Holmes Cathrall)
- Stage 3 (age 22-25): pro tennis attempt, high-level coaching (thank you, Peter Daub), full-time training, international competition
- Stage 4 (age 25-35ish): peak playing level due to physical stamina, tactical awareness, emotional maturity, competitive experience, and no longer having self-esteem and income tied to tennis outcomes
- Stage 5 (age 35ish-present): steady decline due to age, lack of practice/competition, demands of family and business, marked by occasional leveling-off at moments of renewed interest and/or opportunity to practice and compete
- Stage 6 (unknown timeline): anticipated continuation of steady decline until nursing home or death, hopefully punctuated by a few more leveling-off

periods when nothing hurts too much and I don't get distracted by pickleball

The Word *We*

I frequently met with parents and kids who were thinking of attending our program. At one meeting with a dad and his eleven-year-old daughter something didn't feel right as I observed the uncomfortable body language of the girl sitting quietly in the corner. Her father had started the meeting by describing how much potential he believed his daughter had, but he quickly moved on to describe, in detail, the various issues he had with her game. Every other sentence started with the word we: "We have been playing for five years but don't seem to be able to control our emotions well under pressure." "We have really good ground strokes but don't like to come to the net." "We often get up on our opponents but always seem to let up and end up losing." He spoke as if he were an expert on the game as he listed the skills she needed to develop. I was certain he was right, in some sense. After all, what eleven-year-old doesn't need to improve something? Heck, I'd been playing tennis my whole life and still had lots to work on. It seemed to me he thought tennis was something you could master in a short period of time. I started to understand why his daughter looked so uncomfortable.

I tried to pull the daughter into the conversation by asking her a few questions. The father intercepted each one and answered as he looked intently at her. It was awkward, to say the least.

I stopped him after a few minutes and tried to get him to make eye contact with me. I explained as tactfully as possible that this was a process that would take time. The outcome of that process would work itself out on her timetable, not his. His daughter's improvement had nothing to do with him doing anything. His responsibility would be to provide a positive environment in which she could develop her skills and, hopefully, a love for the sport. But in the end, she should get credit when she improved and take responsibility when she didn't. Through the process of working through challenges on her own, she would develop the confidence and competence needed to become a good player. But more importantly, she'd learn life skills that would apply well beyond the tennis court. He couldn't micromanage his way to successful outcomes for his daughter. He needed to trust the process, give up some control, and let his daughter take some ownership of her tennis experience. For a start, he could let her answer some questions from me.

I knew this was a lot for him to take in. As the discussion continued, I watched the daughter's eyes dart around the room in a mixture of confusion, embarrassment, and boredom. I tried to wrap things up as quickly as possible as the dad continued to talk. My warning against using the word we so much had clearly gone in one ear and out the other; he was back to it within minutes.

As you might guess, I ended up having a limited relationship with this family, as we clearly had some philosophical differences. However, whenever I meet with parents like this, I still do my best to caution them against using the word we. Because if kids get the idea that you, as parents, are co-owners in pursuit of their goals, they become codependent on you. As a result, they never develop a sense of initiative or personal responsibility, qualities that are crucial to success in an individual sport like tennis, not to mention life in general. It's much healthier and more effective for a sports parent to be a facilitator rather than a participant.

CHAPTER 5

What Should I Know about Competition?

(Competition vs. Character)

"Comparison is the thief of joy"

—Theodore Roosevelt

Character and Wiring

I've always thought of character as having to do with mental and moral qualities like self-control, perseverance, work ethic, and mental toughness. And I think we all have the capacity to develop and attain those qualities. However, the degree to which that happens varies from person to person. This has to do with how people are wired, the unique personality traits and temperaments that determine how we process the world around us. In sports, people are wired predominantly in one of three ways: competitive (all about outcomes), performative (more focused on playing than winning), and relational (primarily concerned with relationships). No one falls 100 percent into any of these categories, and there's no specific wiring that ensures success. But I can usually tell which wiring is predominant by what interests a player most. If they love to play points, always know the score, and occasionally make bad line calls, I know they're competition-oriented. If they love to drill, often forget the score, and occasionally make line calls in their opponent's favor, I know they're more performance driven. If they're concerned most about when their friends are coming to practice and love to play doubles, I know they're relationally focused. Each group defines success differently, so it gets complicated if you're a parent or coach. For example, getting a competitive kid to practice more often isn't too difficult if you can connect practicing with a higher likelihood of winning. This is a tougher sell with kids who are performance-or relationship-oriented, because they don't place as high a priority on winning. Everyone might agree that practicing is a good idea, but the motivation, as well as the execution, would vary depending on the wiring of the player.

To complicate things further, every parent has their own wiring, which plays a major part in how they interact with their kids and in how their kids respond. The most frustrated parents are often the ones who are *wired differently than their kids.* An example that comes to mind is that of a dad I dealt with years ago. He came to me concerned that his eleven-year old son, who was primarily performance-oriented, wasn't passionate enough about practicing and competing. He mentioned how competitive, disciplined, and hardworking he was at his job and how frustrating it was that his son wasn't pursuing tennis with the same intensity. The problem was that he hadn't factored in two important considerations. First, equating his approach to his job, as a grown man, with his eleven-year-olds approach to sports was an unreasonable expectation. Second, he hadn't considered how his wiring was different from his kid's. The dad was an outcome-driven, competitive guy whose kid was not wired the same way. I could already see signs that the dad's frustration was projecting onto his kid. This, in turn, made the kid uncomfortable and nervous whenever his dad was around.

I've also known parents who struggle because they are *wired the same as their kids.* Like a married couple with the same personality, things often don't work out well. Two examples come to mind. First is a competitively wired mom with a daughter who was just as competitive. The mom was a constant presence at all her daughter's practices, evaluating her every move. Whenever the kid would hit a bad shot, the mom would react negatively or storm off to the car. The kid was just as intense as her mom, so she had to deal with her own frustration along with her mom's. As you might predict, she was a hypertensive bundle of nerves who was rarely relaxed enough to play to her full potential. Her mom never saw the connection.

Around the same time we had another mom/daughter combination who were on the other end of the spectrum. To them, tennis was all about having fun (performance) and making friends (relational). The mom rarely watched lessons or clinics, had little to no input in her daughter's tennis life, and never held her daughter to a high standard. The problem was that the daughter was quite talented and had potential that wasn't being realized. She could have benefited from her mom gently pushing her to focus, work harder, and compete with a bit more intensity. Since the mom wasn't wired competitively, this never occurred to her.

The point here is that to be effective as a sports parent, you have to be aware of both your kid's wiring and your own. Sometimes it's best to think counterintuitively rather than defaulting to what feels right based on your own wiring. Parents wired differently than their kids can benefit from putting themselves in their kids' shoes rather than expecting them to walk in theirs. Parents wired the same as their kids can benefit from stepping out of their comfort zones, because if they don't, their kids never will. It's OK for a competitive parent to take their foot off the gas sometimes, just as it's OK for a performance- or relationship-oriented parent to step on the gas occasionally.

Competing and Comparing

Years ago, I heard a presentation from a well-known sports psychologist who argued that the two most challenging sports psychologically were tennis and boxing. The main difference between the two, he noted, is that you never see a boxer pout, whine, or argue with the referee (all behaviors tennis players are well known for), because any negativity results in being punched in the face. The main similarity is that both sports are individual and competitive, which often leads to an unhealthy preoccupation with the players comparing themselves to one another. A variation of that latter characteristic is sports parents comparing their kids to other kids.

This is an easy trap to fall into. It's hard to know how much to focus on yourself versus how much to focus on your opponent, particularly in an individual sport. The sports psychologist proposed that a player mentally frame a tennis match as a *competition against himself or herself.* Your toughest opponent will usually be you. This makes sense, since you can only control what's happening on your side of the court. However, I think a case can be made that it's helpful to be aware of the tactics that give you the best chance to win. In order to do that, you have to *compare your skills to your opponent's*. Players and parents can understandably struggle balancing this out. Here are a few of the ways people in the tennis world approach the competing/comparing dynamic, for better or worse:

1. *Unproductive external focus:* This is the most common in junior tennis. I once stopped by at a tournament to watch a student of mine play (a young lady around fourteen) and was immediately struck by how intently the girl's parents were watching the match. Her dad was positioned next to the court charting the match on a phone app. He shared the data with me, focusing on where his daughter's stats compared unfavorably to that of her opponent's. Her mom was sitting in a lawn chair right behind the court with eyes riveted to her daughter's every move. Her main concern was that her daughter's forehand seemed less powerful than her opponent's. She asked if I could make it a priority that the issue be addressed in future lessons. Neither parent had noticed that their daughter was winning easily. She was more consistent, had more technical skills overall, and competed better than her opponent. They were focused mostly on the other player, which blinded them to the dynamics of the match. This made it hard, if not impossible, for them to offer constructive feedback to me or their daughter.

2. *Unproductive internal focus:* Parents like the ones mentioned above can get overinvolved and obsessive. When they turn their focus away from others (external) and onto their own kid (internal), things can get just as dysfunctional. The first match I ever played

in a tournament, around age thirteen, was against a guy named Steve. He showed up late, walking ahead of his mom who was carrying a stack of his racquets in one arm and his water cooler in the other. She seemed quite preoccupied with Steve and his needs. Neither Steve nor his mom acknowledged my presence. He was a highly ranked player and no. 1 seed in the tournament, so I guess they figured I posed no threat. Steve looked at his mom obsessively after every point, and his mom's eyes were glued to his every move. Even though Steve won the match, he had emotional meltdowns—swearing, racquet throwing, and so on—whenever a few points went my way. His mom remained supportive and attentive, while seemingly oblivious of his behavior and its negative impact on his performance. The match was much closer than it should have been. Steve and his mom were so preoccupied with themselves that they failed to respect me as an opponent, which is never a good idea when competing with anyone, regardless of their skill level.

3. *Productive external focus:* The core strategy in tennis is to maximize your strengths and exploit your opponent's weaknesses. To do this, you have to spend some time comparing your skill sets to your opponents, that is, you have to focus on the other person. Years ago, I played a match against a guy named Brent. I had

scouted Brent's game going in and knew that he was a stronger player. He had a world-class serve and was extremely talented. I also noticed, however, that he was sometimes undisciplined and prone to mental lapses. As we warmed up, I reminded myself to stay calm, focused, and disciplined. I needed to hit the shots I was capable of instead of trying to match his spectacular winners. I won the first set due to some mindless unforced errors on Brent's part. Unfortunately for me, he started to pay attention and the next two sets ended in his favor. Studying my opponent had enabled me to devise a reasonable strategy and compete well against a stronger player. This, in a sense, was a win for me even though I lost the match.

4. *Productive internal focus:* My wife, Liz, was valedictorian of her high school class. A few years ago, she shared one of her core principles for competing academically. Identify the kid who made the best grades and work hard enough to beat that kid. She called this chasing the rabbit. Around that same time, I was catching up with a former student, John, who was trying to make his college tennis team. He said he had observed the habits of the best players on the team and resolved to work 10 percent harder than those guys. John not only made the team that year but had the best winning percentage. The best players on the team had become

his rabbits, which he used as motivation to excel in athletics just as Liz had in academics.

The best example I know when it comes to balancing the competition/comparison dynamic successfully is Rafael Nadal. In pre-match interviews, he consistently mentions the same three things. First, when asked about his next opponent he is quick to respectfully acknowledge him and says, "He is a very good player"—even if Nadal has beaten the guy numerous times in the past. It's clear that he's put some thought into the tactics most likely to succeed against that player. Second, Nadal mentions that "I will have to play my best to win." This is a subtle but powerful way of saying he expects to win if he plays well—confidence and humility at the same time. Lastly, he always ends by saying, "I will try my best"—and anyone who has ever watched Nadal play knows that this, more than anything, defines him as a competitor.

Notice that two of these three comments have to do with Nadal (internal) rather than his opponent (external). This, I think, is a good formula for success—simple but profound. Nadal's results certainly speak for themselves.

The Discipline of Character

"The search for truth is important not because reaching it is guaranteed—there are no such guarantees—but as a discipline of character."[1] This statement by law professor Anthony T. Kronman caught my eye because substituting the phrase *competitive success* for *truth* in it sums up my entire perspective on sports. *The pursuit of competitive success and the discipline of character that results will ultimately be more valuable than competitive success itself.* Here are a couple of stories to illustrate.

The first is from a player's perspective. The best tennis shot I ever hit was at a men's open tournament on an indoor court in Buffalo, New York, when I was seventeen years old. At one point in the match, my opponent came to the net, so I lobbed over his backhand side. He jumped up, snapped his wrist, and hit a backhand overhead, which angled sharply cross court. I noticed the ball was bouncing fairly high, so I started running full speed in hopes of getting to it before it landed on the next court. I can count on one hand the number of times I have ended up on an adjacent court in order to chase down a shot. I arrived there just before the ball hit the ground and somehow managed to hit it back at an even sharper angle. My opponent reached out, but the ball got past him. As it landed, I heard a loud gasp from the crowd upstairs and pounding on the glass that separated the courts from the viewing area. After many years of playing tennis, I can't remember ever hitting a better shot.

---

[1] Anthony T. Kronman, *The Downside of Diversity* (Wall Street Journal August 2, 2019).

Unfortunately, in tennis, great shots are only worth one point. Even though I had tried my hardest, I lost the match. I felt as if I had let my parents and coach down. I could hardly speak afterwards. What confused me was why the people whose opinions I cared about most, my parents and coach, were so upbeat. They talked about what a great match it was and how proud they were of my attitude and effort. Clearly there was a major disconnect here. All I cared about was the competition. I didn't realize at the time that they were far more interested in my character.

The second story is from a parent's perspective. Recently I ran into the dad of two kids I had coached in the early years of the junior academy I directed. His kids had long since graduated college, but as we exchanged small talk, I was reminded of the past. When he'd first brought his kids to us, he commented on how professionally our program was run and how pleased he was that they had found such a good home in which to train. As time passed, the issues that always seemed to appear when working with the parents of high-level juniors arose: concerns about who his kids got to practice with at clinic, whether I would be able to attend matches at tournaments, scheduling convenient lessons times, and more. Over the next few years, they bounced back and forth to various programs, including ours, but never stayed in one place for too long. From my perspective, he was sacrificing the good in search of the perfect. However, now that his kids were grown, all those concerns seemed to be forgotten. He talked now, in retrospect, about how thankful he was that tennis had prepared his kids for success in life. The time management skills, personal discipline, and work ethic they had developed were all pivotal in their personal and professional lives.

As I recall both of these stories, I can't help but think about how similar I was at seventeen to this dad during his kids' junior tennis years. Neither one of us could see the forest for the trees. My losing a tennis match was just as inconsequential as whether that dad ever found the perfect tennis program for his kids. We acted according to what we understood and cared most about at the time. But years later, we both came to the same conclusion. In sports, the concerns that occupy your mind in the moment rarely turn out to matter much later on. What matters in the end are the relationships you build, the memories you make, and, most importantly, the character you develop. It's all about discipline of character—work ethic, perseverance, and sportsmanship—because that's what lasts. It's OK if everything else fades away.

Chapter 6

Do I Have to Be as Intense as the Other Parents?

(Sprint vs. Marathon)

"If I've learned nothing else, it's that time and practice equals achievement."

—Andre Agassi

"What Are the Chances of These Kids Becoming Pros?"

The father of one of our young players (a boy of around ten) asked me that question one day as he watched a clinic for our older, more advanced kids. At first I thought he was joking. From my perspective, pro tennis was such a remote possibility that I rarely, if ever, considered it. This dad was a tennis enthusiast who had recently moved from an Eastern

European country where, he explained, sports are seen as a way of moving up in the world—this included pro tennis. I sensed that, to him, the kids in clinic didn't look much different than the pros he watched on TV. Therefore, it wasn't unreasonable to expect that some of those kids, including his son, might become pro tennis players.

I started off by explaining that the kids he was watching were mostly good high school players. Some were successful at the state and regional level. This was a small pond of players relative to the vast ocean of kids playing junior tennis worldwide. When exposed to international competition, the kids in clinic would look much less impressive. Second, I pointed out that kids who have a chance to play professionally devote themselves exclusively to tennis. None of the kids he was watching were living that lifestyle. The comforts and options that American kids have make it easy to get distracted from such a singular focus.

I explained that to be reasonably successful in tennis, you have to be competent in four areas: physical, technical, strategic, and emotional. In pro tennis, however, you need to be strong in all four areas and exceptional in one or two; weakness in any of them eliminates the possibility of professional success. I used some examples of players I figured he had in mind—Roddick's world class serve and forehand, Nadal's incredible physical and emotional stamina, Federer's ballet-like movement and athleticism. Very few players develop skills like these.

I told him that it's hard, if not impossible, to predict which kids will make it at any level—junior, college, or pro. Every player is unique. Timing and good fortune also have a part to play. Success only comes at the intersection of preparedness and opportunity. There are many other variables as well—physical development, emotional maturity, mental toughness, family dynamics, genetics, injuries, burnout, and life balance issues, just to name a few.

Finally, I thought it might be helpful to mention that pro tennis has different meanings depending on who you're talking to. My definition of a pro tennis player is a person who can support him- or herself financially by playing tennis.[1] I explained that when I played in the 1980s the top two hundred players in the world were, generally speaking, at the break-even point—that is, where prize money would offset the expenses of travel, coaching, equipment, and so on (a quick Google search revealed it remains around that number today). Even as a former top player for a Division 1 college, I was never able to reach that point. There are very few professions this exclusive. I told him to imagine a world where engineers, which was his vocation, were ranked

---

[1] I also mentioned that he would probably run into teaching pros who included on their resume that they played pro tennis (myself included). That means they were good enough to compete somewhere, at some time, in a tournament where there was prize money involved and, possibly, ATP (Association of Tennis Professionals) computer ranking points at stake. This does not mean that you made it as a pro player by my definition.

worldwide. If only a couple hundred were ranked high enough to make a living, there would be far fewer engineers in the world.

The bottom line was that pro tennis wasn't impossible for these kids, just extremely improbable. Regardless of that, they would each receive benefits from playing tennis that make it well worthwhile: a healthy lifestyle, stronger character, quality relationships, and a chance to learn a sport they could enjoy throughout their lives. In addition, many kids in the United States have access to training programs, a well-developed junior tournament system, and the opportunity to play college tennis. His son was fortunate to live in a country where he could take advantage of the benefits tennis would provide, regardless of whether it resulted in a pro career.

As I reflected on this discussion, I hoped I hadn't discouraged this dad too much. He was a well-meaning guy who wanted to provide an opportunity for his son. But he seemed like a sprinter staring at the finish line only a hundred yards away. When the race started, he would be running as fast as he could. But a sprinter's pace can't be maintained for long. Sports mirror life; they're more a marathon than a sprint. Marathoners can't see the finish line, so they simply focus on running at a pace they can sustain. I hoped my chat with this kid's dad led him toward the latter approach. There was no need, at this point, to focus too much on the finish line.

Finish Lines

Years ago I went to see Jennifer, a girl I'd been working with for a few years, play in her first big tournament at the state level. She was around ten or eleven years old. Matched up against a more experienced and bigger opponent, she was understandably anxious. Her dad looked a bit nervous as well, although he tried not to show it. Jennifer's opponent hit harder, but Jennifer was quicker, more consistent, and composed. As a result, I knew she would win easily, and she did.

Jennifer and her dad were excited; they were getting their first taste of a sports-induced high that can be addictive. It puts everyone in a good mood and makes the future look bright. They had lots of questions for me after the match, all focused on the next twenty-four hours: What time would I be there the next day? Could I warm her up for her match? Did I know anything about her next opponent? On the basis of one big win, they had gone into sprint mode, characterized by an intense focus on what's happening right now and pursuing that next big win. It's an urgent sense that the finish line is just ahead and you need to run as fast as you can. The problem is that competitive sport is a marathon that takes a long time to run. No matter how well you do, there's always something to do next, always another finish line.

I remember having mixed emotions. I felt it likely that Jennifer was going to be very successful as a tennis player. She had so many qualities that pointed in that direction—passion, intensity, talent, competitiveness, work ethic. But I also knew there were unforeseen challenges, like the time and money that would need to be spent by her parents, the emotional toll from the heartbreaking losses that often come after every big win, and the strain in family dynamics associated with so much focus needing to be placed on one kid. There was no way to predict whether the benefits would outweigh the costs. It felt like I was watching people drive down a highway on a sunny day towards a storm that only I could see.

When you start out as a player or a player's parent, you simply don't know what you don't know. The tendency is to focus on what feels good at the moment—winning matches, getting ranked, and so on. Kids like Jennifer who win in the early years (around the ages of eight through twelve) usually have two dominant qualities: consistency and competitiveness. However, long term success is dependent on building skills that young kids rarely have: aggressive ground strokes, volleys/overheads, tactical awareness, and mental toughness. These skills are often overlooked at this stage, particularly if the kids are winning with the skills they already have. It's hard to sell kids, and sometimes their parents, on risking short-term results for long-term development.

To win competitive tennis matches, a kid needs to be fully invested emotionally, mentally, and physically. Like a sprinter looking down the track at the finish line, they have to stay in the moment. But to be successful in future races, it's often helpful to think more like a marathon runner. This is where parents come in. They don't have to play the matches, so they have the luxury of being able to detach and focus on the big picture. It's like bringing a new baby home from the hospital as a first-time parent. There are lots of important things to think about in the short term, but it's also a good time to start planning how to pay for their college education. Parents are obviously in the best position to strike this balance. It's OK if the kids have more of a sprinter's perspective. Parents need to have the marathon in mind as well.

I remember listening, back in the 80s, to John McEnroe being interviewed after finishing the year as the no. 1 player in the world. The interviewer asked how he planned to spend his off-season. McEnroe responded that he was heading back to work with his coach on improving his fundamentals. Years later I listened to an interview with Rafael Nadal after losing a heartbreaking match at the US Open. He said he was planning on getting back to work with his coaches to figure out how to "solve the problem." Regardless of the outcomes, both players were focused on moving forward and continuing to improve. They were neither overconfident nor discouraged. They had learned to balance the intensity of the sprint with the demands of the marathon. That's a tough perspective to acquire and it's why it's hard for professional players (let alone juniors) to succeed over many years. It's a perspective that's developed through years of experience and the support of parents and coaches who understand the sprint vs. marathon dichotomy.

Within a few years, Jennifer was one of the top-ranked players in the country. By the time she was eighteen, she had received multiple scholarship offers to play tennis at Division 1 colleges. There were many ups and downs on that journey. My intention, as I walked along with her and her family, was to encourage her parents to think more about how they would define success in the big picture rather than Jennifer's achieving specific outcomes—winning a tennis match, attaining a college scholarship, turning pro, getting ranked no. 1, and so on. I knew they could easily get distracted from what should be their primary goal, which was creating an environment in which Jennifer could achieve her goals in the short term while developing good character, learning life skills, and building quality relationships in the long term. Jennifer's junior career was a successful one by any standard, but more importantly, she grew up into a good person. Her parents' ability to keep a balanced perspective was one of the main reasons for that.

Rationalizations and Regrets

As I've observed sports parents and reflected on my own experiences as a parent, the same themes keep recurring in the context of the sprint vs. marathon mentality. While my daughters were growing up, I thought I was in a sprint starting when they were born and ending when they shipped off to college. I rationalized that there was limited time to get the job done and that my actions would have significant consequences. This, of course, was true to some degree. I realize now that parenting is more of a marathon. It's not over when your kids move out of the house; it simply moves to another phase. Parenting wasn't the pressure-packed, intense, and urgent sprint that I initially made it out to be. This was much easier to see in hindsight.

I try to keep that in mind when I'm dealing with sports parents. I understand how easy it is to rationalize the sprinters mentality, particularly in a culture that celebrates sports achievement as much as ours. Below I've listed some reasons parents get pulled into the sprint mindset, followed by some principles for those who would rather run a marathon.

Rationalizations for running the sprint

1. Living vicariously through the kids
   Years ago, I knew a dad who was obsessed about his son's tennis achievements. It was as if he had connected his success in life with his kid's success on a tennis court. This struck me as a recipe for dysfunction. It's far better to be proud of your kid for their achievements than to be proud of yourself for having a kid who achieves.

2. Desire to control
   One of the funniest, and saddest, comments I have received was from a mom who asked me if I could "wash his brain"—referring to her desire that her sixteen-year-old son pursue tennis with more passion. Sometimes, though, it's better to let your kid be who they are rather than force them to be someone else.

3. Unrealistic expectations
   I've already mentioned the dad of an eleven-year-old boy who told me, regarding his son's tennis, "I just want him to take pride in what he does like I do at my job." That's a heck of a stretch for an eleven-year-old. Junior tennis is a *game*, not a profession. Expecting it to be more than that will lead to frustration for the kid and disappointment for the parent.

4. Equating early success with long-term achievement
   At a tournament I once watched a talented nine-year-old girl, whom I coached, being interviewed by a local newspaper. Her parents acted as if it was the beginning of a career in pro tennis. Unfortunately early success in junior tennis rarely correlates to becoming a pro tennis player.

5. Not falling behind
   I once coached a thirteen-year-old girl who had earned a high national ranking. Although many of her peers lived and trained at academies, she chose to continue to train at home. It was a tough decision but turned out to be the right decision for her. There is no single template that guarantees success. Better to think through what's right for you rather than try to keep up with others.

Principles for running the marathon

1. Establish good patterns early
   The physical habits that kids form early tend to stick. The same holds true psychologically. I can think of many adults who never outgrew the dysfunctional, entitled thought patterns they learned playing sports as a kid. The key principle, as a parent, should be to create an encouraging, supportive environment for your kid without enabling them too much.

2. Give up control
   I think there are basically two worldviews from which you can raise kids. One is based on the worldly perspective that you are ultimately in control of how your kids turn out. The other is based on the spiritual belief

that your kids are essentially on loan from God. The latter enables you to be much less stressed, intense, obsessive, or overinvolved. Ultimate control is an illusion and a trap.

3. Set realistic standards and applaud baby steps
One of my favorite tennis moms once wrote up a contract for her thirteen-year-old son who was struggling with attitude issues. It outlined reasonable standards that focused on incremental improvements. I thought that made sense. No parent looks at a toddler after their first step and says, "It's about time." Instead, they praise the effort and say, "Try again."

4. Avoid "no win" framing
Parents of kids who succeed early in sports often assume that their success will continue indefinitely. This creates a no-win mental environment: success is expected, and setbacks are a disaster. Obviously this is a tough environment for a kid psychologically. It's better to base expectations on challenge rather than fear: success is earned, and setbacks are opportunities.[2]

---

[2] For more on this, I recommend Carol S. Dweck, *Mindset: The New Psychology of Success* (New York: Ballentine, 2006).

5. Challenge the assumptions
   It's a false premise that copying whatever the best kids are doing at the time (homeschooling, academies, immersion in one sport, and so on) produces better results. Learn from others, but don't assume that what's right for someone else is right for you. Accept that there will be potential downsides regardless of which way you go, and that's OK.

I met a physical therapist a few years ago who described herself as a reformed soccer mom. She told me that she had lost perspective during her kids' playing days and regretted being so intense about every little detail. She said that she tended to do what she saw other parents doing, like driving too fast on the highway because everyone else is speeding. In retrospect, she said she would have made a few decisions differently, but her main regret was that she should have had a more relaxed spirit. This mom had the mindset of a sprinter only to realize later she was actually running a marathon, which requires a much different mentality. She had come to the same conclusion I had after my daughters grew up. It would have been better—for both ourselves and our kids—if we both had understood the kind of race we were running right from the start.

Ends of the Spectrum

One Sunday morning, I stopped by at a junior tennis tournament to watch some matches. On the court in front of me there were two fourteen-year-old boys battling it out. I noticed they were questioning most every line call and trash-talking constantly. A monitor from the USTA was stationed at the net post. None of this was unusual but, generally speaking, not a good sign at a junior tournament. What concerned me most was the father of one of the kids standing behind the court. He was looking, to put it mildly, a bit worked up. Within minutes, his kid started arguing with the monitor in the best John McEnroe imitation[3] I had ever seen. His dad was now pacing behind me, looking like he was about to lose it. Unfortunately, his anger seemed directed at the monitor rather than at his out-of-control kid. This was not a good sign either. The monitor gave a point penalty to McEnroe Jr. This prompted McEnroe Sr. to start yelling at the monitor through the fence and give him the finger. A few minutes later the match was over, and it looked like McEnroe Jr. lost. McEnroe Sr. promptly greeted the monitor as he left the court and gave him a verbal

---

[3] For a visual of this, search YouTube for "John McEnroe tantrums." These clips are still entertaining to watch, but I'm sad that his worst moments on a tennis court are recorded for posterity. I certainly wouldn't wish that on anyone, particularly myself. Tennis has a way of bringing out the best and the worst in us all. For what it's worth, I think McEnroe was a truly great player and also is one of the better tennis commentators on TV.

tongue-lashing complete with multiple f-words. The monitor kept his composure but threatened to ban McEnroe Jr. from future tournaments unless McEnroe Sr. would calm down. He finally relented and walked away toward the parking lot, but not before making a few more choice comments just to make sure he got in the last word. To this day I've never seen an uglier scene at a junior tournament.

As I tried to process what I had just witnessed, my attention turned to the court next door, where two other fourteen-year-old boys, Tommy and Stuart, were playing. Both boys had been in our program for years. I had watched them grow up like brothers and knew their families well. I didn't notice if either of their parents were at the match. Unlike McEnroe Sr., these sets of parents liked to stay in the background. Stuart had been beating Tommy in the matches they had played recently, but I could sense the match was close. After a few great points, Tommy won the match with a forehand volley winner and walked toward the net to shake hands. He'd pulled off a big upset. I knew this would be huge for him but really tough for Stuart. I watched carefully to see how they would handle themselves as they came to the net to shake hands. As Tommy reached out his hand, Stuart took it and pulled him into a hug. In the midst of his disappointment, he had the presence of mind to genuinely congratulate his opponent. Tommy, in turn, was gracious in victory. I could tell he was holding in his excitement so as not to show up Stuart. It was a rare display of sportsmanship that provided a sharp contrast to what I had watched in the previous match. In junior tennis, it doesn't get much better than that.

In the span of a few minutes on that Sunday morning, I had witnessed both ends of the spectrum in junior sports. The attitudes and behaviors of the kids could not have been more different. I believe that to be a direct reflection of how they were being raised by their parents.

Watching McEnroe Sr. was like watching a sprinter at a track meet, every match a race that had to be won. All that seemed to matter to him was what he felt at that moment. There was no awareness of the bigger picture. He didn't seem to mind being on center stage; it was as if he thought he was playing the match himself. I couldn't help but wonder how long he would keep that mindset and whether his kid could succeed in such an intense environment. I'd run across a few parents with similar perspectives. They are always around at lessons, clinics, and tournaments. They love to be involved in the details of their kid's tennis. Their emotions swing wildly. And they're quick to intercede to solve problems for their kids but prone to overlooking behavior issues that need to be addressed. Thankfully, most parents grow out of this once they realize they can't maintain that pace long and how counterproductive that approach is in the first place.

Tommy's and Stuart's parents were more like marathoners. They took the wins and losses in stride, because they knew the race was going to last awhile. Although they preferred to stay in the background, I was certain that if either of their kids had behaved like McEnroe Jr., they would have gotten involved quickly and forcefully to control their behavior. Marathon parents like these have lots of energy, just a different kind than sprinter parents. They pay attention but don't obsess. They focus on instilling character in their kids. And they have the discipline to project a calm demeanor even when their emotions are boiling below the surface. As a result, their kids reflect many of the same values and qualities, which serve them well both on the court and off.

Chapter 7

Will This Be Worth the Effort?
(Enablement vs. Independence)

"Being a parent is not transactional. We do not get what we give. It is the ultimate pay-it-forward endeavor: We are good parents not so they will be loving enough to stay with us but so they will be strong enough to leave us ."

—Anna Quindlen

Delusions

The key to improvement is to practice with and play against players who are better than you are. This is a widely accepted premise in sports because, to a large extent, it's true. In junior tennis, it's commonly called *playing up*. But an aphorism often attributed to French philosopher Voltaire applies here, "the perfect is the enemy of the good." You can overdo anything. I like beer and ice cream, but too much of either tends to be a problem. Many parents assume playing up to be an essential part of their kids' experience in tournaments and tennis programs. After all, if their kid can't play with better players, what's the point? To the few parents who ask my opinion on the topic, I say that playing up certainly has its benefits but if you place too much value on playing up it becomes a subtle form of enablement. There's never pressure to perform, because you're always playing with house money—no risk of losing, only the upside of winning. It's easy to get motivated to play someone you consider to be stronger; it's much tougher mentally to play against your peers or those whom you consider weaker. In that sense playing up makes things easier, which can be counterproductive if you're trying to develop accountable, disciplined players. They need to learn to stay focused and play to a high standard regardless of the opponent. The inability to do this explains why kids can't consistently beat the players they *should* beat, that is, less experienced players ranked lower than they are. This is something that many parents have trouble understanding.

Another problem with this premise is that it's predicated on the idea that one player will always be better than another. But sports are like life: the only constant is change. People improve at varying rates over time. Levels of play vary from moment to moment. The idea that there's a static state in which one player is better than another is a delusion. The most common word people with this delusion use is *should*, as in "I should have made that shot," "I should have beaten that player," or "my kid should have won that match." There is no *should*; there is only *did* or *did not* at a given point in time. When you missed, you missed. When you lost, your opponent was better that day. Everything can change tomorrow—or in the next few minutes. The challenge is to respond well when you're playing poorly and maintain high standards when you're playing well. Other people have nothing to do with it. Thinking of others as better or worse is nothing but a distraction from the things that matter, like effort, execution, and engagement. It's not about who your kid is playing; it's about *how* they're playing. It's an approach based on personal responsibility and discipline, which is what most parents want their kids to learn in the first place.

A related delusion in junior tennis is the idea that by associating with successful people, you become more likely to succeed yourself. Many junior tennis programs are based on this premise. People tend to flock to where the "good" kids are. The best way to build a junior program, in the short term at least, is to find a way to attract the best players. That's why those players, and their parents, often get preferential treatment (extra attention from the pros, scholarships to attend the program, and so on). Usually, over time, programs based on this idea fall apart as those good kids leave in search of their own delusions about associating with better players. Again, this idea has merit; there's nothing wrong with wanting to be around successful people. It just needs to be put into perspective.

A better way to think about this is through the concept of ignition. Ignition is the idea that people are powerfully motivated by observing and imitating successful people.[1] There's a fine line between the delusion of association and ignition. It's great to find inspiration from others; it's delusional to think you'll get better simply by being in their presence. At some point you have to do the work yourself. Greatness isn't achieved by people who have a follower mentality. It's about learning from others, taking responsibility for yourself, and working hard to get where you want to go.

Potential

A question parents often ask me is, "Do you think my kid has potential?" This is tough to answer for several reasons. First, it has to do with predicting the future based on a host of variables. Second, it involves dealing with parents who have different expectations, goals, and definitions of potential (potential to do what?). Taking all this into account,

---

[1] For more on this concept, I highly recommend Daniel Coyle, *The Talent Code: Greatness Isn't Born. It's Grown. Here's How.* (New York: Bantam, 2009).

I've found it best to share principles rather than make predictions. My answer has varied widely based on the circumstances and people involved. Here are a few examples.

Character—passion—skill

John's parents, Peter and Susie, left the details of tennis up to John and his coaches. They were primarily interested in two things: John's character (attitude, effort, responsibility, sportsmanship, and so on) and the impact tennis would have on his life overall. As John came toward the end of his junior career, they wanted to know whether I thought John's tennis pursuits should be a factor in his college plans. It was their way of asking, "What's his potential?"

I told them there are three factors that determine success at the college level. The most important factor is character. By any definition of character, John stood out and would likely continue to do so. The second factor is passion. John loved tennis, but most importantly, he owned it. He was responsible, self-motivated, and ambitious. I felt confident his passion would continue throughout his college years. Lastly, talent and skill would obviously play a part. Talent and skill are related but not the same. The distinction is important. John was considering playing Division 1 college tennis. Relative to that pool of competition, his talent was average. The more important consideration was whether his skill level would improve. I had seen many talented college players whose skill level never improved much. College athletics is a four-year process, so what matters isn't where you start but where you finish. Thanks to John's character and passion, I knew his skill level would improve, which meant those two factors were more important than his talent. With all this in mind, I felt confident that John had the potential to do well athletically and that it would be wise to take that into account when choosing a college.

Big fish in small ponds

In a previous chapter, I mentioned a dad who had asked me, "What are the chances of these kids becoming pros?" This was his version of "What's their potential?" I told him that potential is relative to the people you're comparing yourself to. But that's a slippery slope because you can never control other people. In hopes of reframing the discussion, I told him how my dad approached this topic when I was young.

After I became no. 1 on my high school team and started to think of myself as a good tennis player my dad asked me, "Do you want to be a big fish in a small pond or a little fish in a big pond?" He knew I was comparing myself only to the fish in my little pond. I think he believed I had some potential but didn't have any idea what I would, or would not, achieve in tennis. The most important thing to him, I think, was that I stay grounded while maintaining my competitiveness and ambition. My dad had a concise way of teaching subtle but powerful principles.

The first college we visited during my senior year in high school was Penn State University, which was the biggest pond I could conceive of at the time. The coach said he would let me try out for the team but that playing in the top three, which *may* qualify me for *some* scholarship money, would be very unlikely. The next stop on that trip was Lafayette College in Easton, Pennsylvania. The Lafayette coach told me I would likely play no. 1 my first year and offered me a *full* scholarship. I think the scholarship at Lafayette sounded pretty good to my dad. However, within minutes of getting into the car for the drive home, I told him I wanted to go to Penn State. To me it was a no-brainer: bigger pond. Note to parents: Be careful what you teach your kids.

Somehow I made the top three at Penn State my freshman year and by senior year was the no. 1 player. By that time, I was already thinking about the next big pond to swim in, the world of pro tennis. That one question my dad had asked back in high school had set me up to succeed in ponds I couldn't conceive of four years prior. I don't think he spent much time thinking about how much potential I had. He was more interested in teaching me principles for success that would apply on and off the court. My guess is that he trusted the results would take care of themselves.

How fast can the tree grow?

In poker tournaments on TV, the most exciting moment is when the player goes all in, betting all they have on one hand. Kevin's parents were all-in parents. In a well-meaning effort to support him, they spent an inordinate amount of time, money, and energy focused on Kevin's tennis. He had been fairly successful in junior tennis, and his parents were hopeful this would translate into success at the college level. But by age seventeen, Kevin's ranking was not justifying much interest from college coaches and his motivation was starting to drop. His parents came to me concerned that time was running out and he was not living up to his "potential." I assumed that meant, to them, maintaining a high ranking, being recruited to play college tennis, and so on.

I pointed to a tree just outside the window and explained that watching kids develop in sports was like watching a tree grow in the backyard. The more you watch it, the longer it seems to take, but then one day you look up and its shade covers the whole yard without you having done all that much. It's helpful to water the tree occasionally, especially when first planted, but then you have to let nature take its course. I hoped they got the idea that they might be watching their tree too much. The reality was that Kevin had improved and would continue to do so, but he struggled emotionally with the weight of his parents' expectations and overinvolvement. In that environment, the potential of even the most talented player is limited.

The best definition I've heard for potential goes like this: potential is latent ability that may or may not be developed or attained (another saying worthy of a t-shirt). I still have trouble when parents ask me about their kids' potential, because they want a quick answer. This, to me, is an exercise in futility. Potential is latent; sometimes it's easy to spot, sometimes not so much. Either way, it *may or may not* ever be developed or attained. Accepting that can be challenging for parents. It's a parent's responsibility to help their kids develop potential but detrimental to enable them to realize that potential. It's a tricky balance to strike and one of many reasons that sports parenting is a challenging job. Ultimately the kids will have to own their successes and failures. There are lessons to be learned in both.

Responsibility

A few years ago I had the opportunity to stay at one of the nicest, and probably most expensive, private homes I'd ever stayed in. It was located in the foothills of the Rockies and owned by a successful businessman lovingly known to some in his family as Big Dave. He had spent years selecting the site, building the house, and developing the property. The morning we were to leave, I woke to the sound of a snow blower outside my window. I opened the curtain as a team of people was clearing the night's snowfall off the long driveway. As Dave started down the driveway to take us to the airport later that morning, I mentioned how nice it was to have people to clear the snow. He told me he was trying to sell the house, but the maintenance cost, including the guys clearing snow, was enough to scare away most buyers. He didn't seem concerned though; his perspective was that "anyone who cared about the maintenance cost on this house couldn't afford it anyway."

I think of this whenever I talk to tennis parents who give me the impression that they are looking for financial return on their investment in developing their kid's tennis skills, like a college scholarship or a pro career. Like Dave, they've spent, or plan on spending, lots of time, money, and energy on their kid's athletic pursuits—building the house, so to speak. My encouragement to them is to think about investing in sports like Dave thought about his house. Spend what you can afford and trust that things will work out apart from the financial return. There are benefits to owning a home, or investing in sports for your kids, that extend far beyond the monetary considerations.

By my sophomore year in college, I had proven myself enough that the coach offered me some scholarship money to play on the team. Needless to say, I was excited to call home and share the news with my parents. They seemed happy but mentioned they had planned on funding my college education either way. I remember feeling a little confused and disappointed they didn't share my enthusiasm. Years later, as I drove down that long driveway with Dave, I felt like I understood my parents' reaction better. Like Dave investing in his house, my parents' investment in my college education was what they considered "sunk cost" (a term my dad explained to me years later). It was already planned and accounted for. They wanted to provide for my education and had worked hard to do that. They weren't looking for a financial return on their investment, because they knew a college education would have an important impact on my life. There were no strings attached, other than the expectation that I make the most of the opportunities they provided. Parenting to them was more about what they were responsible to give rather than what they got in return.

I shared this concept, years ago, with some parents who were heavily involved in every detail of their son's tennis, investing a lot financially and clearly looking for some kind of tangible result. I remember the mom asking sarcastically, "So you want me not to do anything and let him do whatever he wants, regardless of his results?" But, of course, that's not quite the idea. Parents have a responsibility to provide what they can to support their kids. But kids need to be held accountable for the things that really matter—effort, attitude, sportsmanship, and more. There aren't necessarily tangible outcomes that immediately result from these things. That needs to be OK with you as a parent. There's more value in long-term character development than any short-term result you can measure on a balance sheet (or ranking). Sometimes you have to let the results take care of themselves.

What's the point?

As I've mentioned before, baseball was a big part of my life as a kid. In my town's Little League, most ten-year-olds were placed in the minors division. I knew, however, that a few exceptional ten-year-olds would be put up in the majors with eleven- and twelve-year-old kids based on their performance in try-outs. Although I was barely ten, I believed I was good enough to play with the older boys. My expectation was that if I tried my hardest, had the opportunity to show my skills, and the coaches paid attention, I would likely make the majors. My dad, who had taught me most of what I knew about baseball, wasn't there. He didn't give me any pep talk that morning and barely acknowledged that I was trying out. I know that to many parents today, that might seem odd, particularly since he had invested so much time helping me develop and, I assume, was interested in how things went. I think that he was a product of his generation. I doubt that his dad would have shown up at his baseball try-outs. And I don't think he was emotionally attached either way. He figured he had done his job, so the rest was up to me. I just assumed that's how things worked;

I didn't need my dad watching me from the sidelines for emotional support. For a competitive kid like me, effort wasn't going to be the issue anyway. If anything, my dad's presence would have added fuel to a fire that didn't need any more wood. Growing up like this didn't make me feel less encouraged. It gave me a sense of personal responsibility which has served me well in sports and life.

Even though I felt I had played well in try-outs, the call for the majors never came. I was hugely disappointed and looked to my dad for guidance. He told me that if I wanted to succeed, it wasn't good enough to be a little better than everybody else, I needed to be "head and shoulders" better so that there wasn't the slightest doubt. I was hoping he would call the coach and plead my case. Instead, he encouraged me to work harder and aim to be twice as good at the next opportunity. The message was clear. My success or failure was up to me alone.

This lesson paid off when I tried out for the high school baseball team my freshman year. I had worked really hard at improving my baseball skills but, humbled by my Little League experience, my expectation was to make the junior varsity team with the other kids my age. To my surprise my name was on the list for the varsity team (juniors and seniors). Within my circle of sports buddies, I was an immediate celebrity, even though I sat on the bench all year hoping the coach wouldn't put me in an actual game. I was intimidated by those big juniors and seniors on the field.

In my sophomore year, full of confidence, I went to tryouts assuming I would be guaranteed a spot on the varsity team. Unfortunately, I neglected to hustle (one of my dad's favorite words) like I had as a freshman. The coach cut me—not only from the varsity team, but from the JV team as well. I was crushed. Just like back in Little League, I hoped my dad would call the coach and fix this mistake. He did seem empathetic but, as you might expect, told me I would have to deal with this on my own. After trying for two or three days, I caught up to the coach in his office. He said that I was a good fielder, but my hitting was poor. He didn't elaborate and there was no encouragement to come back the next year and try again. That, essentially, was the end of my baseball career.

Looking back, I learned some painful but powerful lessons. First, never expect anything to be given to me. Second, my nature is to let up unless I discipline myself to hustle 100 percent of the time. Lastly, a chain is only as strong as its weakest link. I spent my time in baseball working on my fielding, which I enjoyed the most, but rarely spent time on improving my hitting. In baseball you need to be good in both fielding and hitting. I was overconfident about my strongest links and ignored my weakest—a bad combination.

Over the next few years, I found a new sport to play: tennis. Within two years I was the best player on my high school team, thanks largely to my athletic experience in baseball and a great high school tennis coach who took special interest in me. Thank you, Mr. McMahon!, still getting used to calling you Terry.

Twenty years later, I asked Mr. McMahon why he spent so much time helping me. He told me it was due to my attitude and dedication—my hustle. My dad had wired work ethic, discipline, and personal responsibility into my system by letting me fail. This, I realize, may seem counterintuitive to many parents today. However, if my parents hadn't let me fail at baseball, I may never have taken up tennis, which, in retrospect, was clearly a better path. I knew my parents cared even when they didn't rescue me. To them, sport was a way to develop my character. That was more important than how anyone felt at any point in the process.

So why tell all these stories so many years later? Who really cares about my glory days playing sports? Absolutely no one—and that's the whole point. Whatever I achieved athletically faded quickly into distant memory. Who I became through sports has lasted my whole life. Sports provided an environment for me to develop character and an opportunity for my parents to shape that character. *Understanding this is essential to being a good sports parent.*

I've heard that sports don't form character; they reveal it. I suppose there may be some truth to that. What I know for certain is that character is the only thing that matters after athletic triumphs and disasters are long forgotten. Achievement in sports is a means to that end, not the end in itself.

Epilogue

As I reviewed the journals that were the genesis of this book, I came across the first note I wrote on the topic of sports parenting. It was written in December of 1997 in the form of a letter composed amidst a cloud of confusion, frustration, and sense of inadequacy. I planned to send it to the parents of a thirteen-year-old girl named Jennifer whom I had been working with since she was nine or ten. My intention was to inform them that I could no longer continue as her coach.

One of the problems with sending that letter was that Jenn's parents were great folks. Both highly intelligent, capable people who loved and cared deeply for her. They loved tennis themselves, so I taught them lessons as well. One of my fondest memories is of Jenn's dad, Jett, at our eight a.m. Saturday lessons in midwinter, when the temperature hadn't yet risen above freezing. When I would arrive to open up the front gate at 7:45, Jett would already be parked on the side of the road. He would already be down to his tennis shorts, just returning from his warm-up jog, steam rising from his baseball cap. This was my kind of guy. As we started each of his lessons, we would review whatever had come up with Jenn's tennis that week. No matter how much Jett wanted to hit, Jenn always came first—a beautiful metaphor for how he approached parenting.

Since Jennifer had become one of the best players in the country, tennis was a big part of her parents' life. One can't happen without the other. That meant I was spending quite a bit of time with Jenn's parents, discussing upcoming matches, deconstructing matches just played, attending to the logistical details of training, coordinating with specialists (sports psychologist, fitness trainer, other coaches). By the time I wrote this note, I was getting pretty stressed out. Even great parents with the best of intentions can lose perspective and start putting plans before principles, form before substance. At the time, I felt Jenn's parents were tipping too far toward the wrong side of many of the dichotomies I've described in this book. So much of what they were preoccupied with wouldn't matter in the big picture. This, I felt, unnecessarily raised everyone's stress level and wasted a lot of time, particularly mine. If this was going to be a marathon, I didn't feel like I would have the energy or inclination to finish. Also, I internalized many of their questions and concerns as a lack of trust in my abilities. A voice in my head would often say, "Why can't you guys relax and just trust me?" On the other hand, I knew they must have trusted me, or I wouldn't be coaching Jenn in the first place. I didn't want to let them down, but I couldn't see how I could continue coaching Jenn much longer. I suppose this internal conflict also contributed to my stress level.

When I look back on this letter now, I realize how judgmental its tone was. It was the ramblings of an immature tennis pro looking for the easy way out. Also, to use some tired clichés, it strikes me that we were all in the same boat, neither seeing the forest for the trees, focused on the urgent rather than the important, sweating the small stuff. This, I suppose, is what often happens when you are inexperienced at anything (coaching or parenting). It would have been unfair to send that letter to Jenn's parents. Thankfully, I never did.

However, it did seem at the time that the only logical path was to meet with Jenn's parents and, as tactfully as I could, tell them we just weren't a good fit. There were a few problems with this. First, quitting is not in my DNA. Second, when I wasn't in this stressed-out state, I genuinely enjoyed coaching Jennifer and truly liked her parents. Lastly, something just didn't *feel* right. I couldn't put my finger on it.

Now I'm usually skeptical of people who say God told them to do this or that. And up to that point, I had never prayed about coaching kids or dealing with their parents. This, however, seemed like a good time to start. I asked for guidance, wisdom, and direction as to what to do. My belief was (and is) that if you sense God telling you to do something, you should do it; if he's telling you not to do something, you shouldn't do it; but if you can't figure out what he's telling you to do, wait. In this case, I sensed that "other larger, stronger, quieter life" (recall the C.S. Lewis quote I mentioned at the beginning of this book) telling me to just . . . wait. So that's what I did.

About six weeks passed until one Saturday afternoon in early February when I came home from teaching, took one look at my wife, and knew something was very wrong. She had just gotten a call informing us Jett had died that morning of a massive heart attack. He was in Chicago with Jennifer at a tournament, had gone for a run that morning, and collapsed in his hotel lobby. Mary Ellen, Jenn's mom, was on her way to Chicago, but asked that I come over when she and Jenn got back in town late that night. All my silly, self-absorbed concerns from December were quickly forgotten. The lonely drive over to their house around midnight, and that visit, are stuck in my memory. There were, and are, no words. To this day, walking with them through that time, and through the next few years, was one of the hardest and most significant things I've ever done as a tennis coach. You just don't think of this stuff when you sign up for the job.

As I write over twenty years later, it's surprising how vivid those memories are. Clichés like "time flies" and "God works in mysterious ways" come to mind. But words have limits. I'll just say I've learned a lot about life from this family, and I'm thankful for answered prayers. It's been inspirational and humbling to be a part of their lives. Over the next years, Jenn stuck with tennis and earned a scholarship to play at the University of Notre Dame. She went on to have a successful business career and, as I write this, she is married with her third child on the way. We still talk when we can, our conversations last a while. Her mom has remarried and continues to be an example of perseverance and faith to those who know her story.

Since I'm in a reflective mood, I just dove into my storage closet and pulled out my file on Jennifer. It's thick with notes from her parents, sports psychologists, trainers, and other coaches. There are lesson plans, letters, performance goals for matches, and a copy of what I said at her dad's funeral. But that's in the past; I haven't looked at that file for years. I just spoke with Jenn recently and none of our discussion had anything to do with tennis. The things we talk about now are much more important: kids, marriage, career, life balance, spirituality, and more. But our time together when she was playing tennis formed the basis for our relationship today. And the lessons she learned through tennis formed much of who she has become as a person. There was a much bigger narrative at work. This is crucial to keep in mind as parents—and, I suppose, a good thought on which to end this book.

Appendix 1:
Terms and Expressions

Junior sports has its own language, much of which doesn't make sense to the uninitiated. Here are a few definitions for terms and expressions you're likely to hear.

General sports

coach: In athletics, any time a person is in a position of authority we call them *coach*. I'm not sure whether this is good or bad, not that anyone's asked me. I think a case could be made, in tennis at least, that we should only use the term to refer to teaching pros who are certified by the United States Professional Tennis Association or Professional Tennis Registry, both of which train and certify tennis pros. That being said, I've known some great coaches who were not certified. Coaching is about making a positive impact regardless of credentials. I've seen high school kids who were helping teach clinics make more of an impact than experienced pros (myself included). People learn in all kinds of ways, from all kinds of people—including their parents, and there's no certification for parenting. It's good for a coach to be certified but it's not a disqualifier if they're not.

APPENDIX 1

academy: When we started Charlotte Tennis Academy in 1989, the idea was to build an instructional program focused exclusively on juniors at all levels between the ages of six and eighteen. The word *academy* sounded good, so we went with it. But it's a catch-all term and has many usages in the sports world. There are programs where kids go to live and train full-time. The goal, usually, is for the kids to play in college or even play professionally. There is an academic component (modified school hours, online school, or home school), but clearly the priority is athletic training. Programs like this are referred to as academies, as well. Many junior programs will label a specific group of kids "academy players" as a way to distinguish them from kids who aren't so advanced or committed. There's nothing wrong with this; labels have their uses. But the bottom line is that within any program there will always be a range of skill levels. Bottom line for parents: find a program that has players who are compatible with your kid, with a schedule that fits your needs, and with quality coaches running the show. What it's called doesn't matter all that much.

moving up: This is a term used in sports programs to describe a player who is deemed ready to play in a group of stronger, older, or more experienced players. From a player or parent perspective, moving up feels great. From a coach's perspective, it's complicated for a few reasons. First, unless the player is head-and-shoulders above the level of the group he is presently in, taking him out of that group means that others who are close in skill level are left behind. This often leaves those players feeling either discouraged or discriminated against. Another downside is that the kid who moves up often gets complacent. They finally made it, so there's less intensity about practicing and improving. On the other hand, moving up can provide a sense of accomplishment and confidence that serves as a powerful motivator. If you are a sports parent, sooner or later your kid will have to deal with one side or the other of this issue.

Tennis specific

Davis Cup: This is an annual international team tennis competition involving the best players from each country, usually their top pros. When I played in college, we often played teams that included players from different countries. Often, before a match, one of my teammates would come up and say, "Yo, be ready. I just heard the guy you're playing was on the [obscure country name] Davis Cup team." Naturally I assumed the guy was an awesome player, got psyched out before I even stepped on the court, and got my butt kicked. With experience, I realized a few things. First, sometimes (but not always) the player in question just knew a guy on the Davis Cup team or practiced once with the guy or took a set off him when they were twelve or . . . you get the idea. Second, even if the guy did play for Swaziland's Davis Cup team, he wasn't any better or worse than the guys I usually played. There was no need to get all worked up.

The same dynamic will be in play when a friend of your kid (or their parent) comes up at a tournament and says, "Hey, I just heard you're playing [player name] who just beat so-and-so yesterday or just won such-and-such tournament last week. You *better be ready!*" Tennis is a hotbed for rumor, gossip, and innuendo—most of it fun and well-meaning, of course. Ignore all of it. I suggest that when your kid is exposed to this silliness, tell them to simply focus on playing to the best of their ability, just like they always should.

treeing: This a term used often when I played juniors years ago, but I haven't heard kids use it much these days. It refers to the *perception* that another player, usually an opponent, played (or is playing) far above their usual level. You might say to your friend at a tournament, "Yeah, I lost, but the guy really treed out of his mind." The implication is that you lost only because you happened to play the guy on a day he was playing exceptionally well—he got lucky. Of course, this is simply a way to save face. It's also dishonest and/or delusional. If your kid starts using this word, wash their mouth out with soap.

indirect wins: This one was always a favorite with me and my buddies in the juniors. Indirects, as we used to call them, work like this. I play a guy—let's call him Joey—and

I win the match. My friend finds out that last week Joey beat Thomas who is ranked no. 1 in the country. In effect, therefore, I have an indirect win over Thomas because I beat Joey who, we heard, beat Thomas. Does that make sense? It sure as heck did to us. We used to spend considerable amounts of time discussing indirect wins. I remember once concocting an indirect win over John McEnroe, at the time no. 1 in the world, because I beat a guy who beat a guy who beat McEnroe when they were both ten years old. Indirect wins apply across age groups, genders, time, and multiples of players. If you work at it hard enough, even a club player today can figure out how they have an indirect over Federer. It's a fun game that passes the time waiting to go on the court at tournaments. It has no connection to reality whatsoever. If you find your kid playing it with their friends, ignore it if they are just having fun. If they are serious, seek professional help.

pusher: This is mostly a derogatory term that tennis players use for another player whose game is based on consistency, fitness, and patience. Pushers rarely hit winners but never miss. They rely on their opponent's errors to win and generally derive a great deal of satisfaction from watching their opponents have mental breakdowns. The truth is that players with this game style are very good players. Consistency is fundamental in tennis. And pushers have figured out how to keep the ball in play more than their opponents.

Therefore they win often; it's just that simple. Pushers are not evil, just devious (and I mean that as a compliment). Like so many terms in tennis, this one is based on a combination of cluelessness, delusion, and arrogance based in insecurity. For example, you overhear your kid say to their friend, "Yeah, I lost, but they were just a pusher and I only play well against players who *hit* the ball." If you hear your kid talking like this, whack them upside their head immediately. If you find yourself making excuses for your kid along these lines, have your kid whack you upside the head.

college tennis: This is a catch-all term used in junior tennis to refer to a fantasy world where everyone is great at tennis and school is free. The truth is there are many levels of college tennis (various divisions of four-year colleges, two-year junior colleges, club tennis, and so on), and scholarships are rare. It does help to be good at tennis to play any level of college tennis, meaning your kid better be fairly committed as a junior (playing four to six times a week, taking lessons and clinics, training on their own, playing tournaments, earning a ranking, and so on).

Occasionally I run across a kid (or their parent) who say they want to play college tennis, but the kid has limited skills, no experience, and rarely plays—since they also want to be their class valedictorian, become a world-class violinist, volunteer at the food bank, and be president of three clubs at school . . . *or* they would simply prefer hanging out with friends. This is an example of expectations exceeding reality which, inevitably, results in disappointment. The goal is to find the best fit for your kid, considering all the factors involved: location, cost, academics, athletic skills, commitment, and so on.

Generally speaking, if your kid is between eight and thirteen years old, it's OK if they just think about college tennis in a nebulous way. After that, it's good to start contacting college coaches and learning about college athletics in general. As in most things, the perception and the reality of college tennis are two different things, so it's best to start educating yourself by the time your kid is a freshman or sophomore in high school. For those who can afford it, there are consultants who specialize in guiding families through the recruiting process. But with some effort, it can be done on your own. Years ago, one of our parents did a comprehensive study of this process. He came up with a plan, executed it, and was instrumental in helping his daughter attain a full scholarship to college. Years later he ended up writing a book on junior tennis. For those interested in checking it out, I recommend Jack Marion's *Junior Tennis for Parents . . . A Sweat Equity Approach!* (Amazon, 2020).

on the tour: Term often used by players, usually just out of college, who are trying their hand at the pro tour. It's a lot of playing tournaments in far-away cities against very good players for little prize money in relative obscurity. The players you see on TV represent the very small tip of the iceberg i.e. players "on the tour".

When I tried my hand at playing on the tour, my girlfriend (now wife, Liz) decided she would travel to Barcelona, Spain, on a break from college to join me for a week. Aside from the obvious allure of spending time with me, I knew she envisioned a vacation complete with beaches, nice restaurants, and tours of the city. Fearing she would be disappointed, I told her not to come. Thankfully, she ignored me and flew over anyway. She spent the week staying in a youth hostel, eating pizza at the same restaurant every night, traveling back and forth to the practice courts, and doing laundry. On the bright side, she was a rock star with all the guys, since she was the only female around. Also, since she could cut hair and none of us had a haircut in months, she opened up shop and made some extra cash. Liz didn't hit any beaches before she returned home. But I know we were both glad she ignored my advice and made that trip.

The best essay I've ever read on the realities of pro tennis is David Foster Wallace's "Tennis Player Michael Joyce's Professional Artistry as a Paradigm of Certain Stuff about Choice, Freedom, Limitation, Joy, Grotesquerie, and Human Completeness."[1] (How's that for a title?) Highly

---

[1] It's included in Wallace's collection of essays, *String Theory: David Foster Wallace on Tennis* (New York: Library of America, 2016).

recommended whether you are a tennis fan or not. If you've never read DFW, you're in for a treat.

Bottom line: playing on the tour sounds glamorous and people are usually impressed when you mention it at parties, but it's not anywhere close to what people think. Ironically, players who barely scratch the surface of pro tennis often make a big deal about it later in life. My friend Pender made it well beyond scratching the surface, into the top one hundred players in the world. Trust me, this is quite an accomplishment. I've never heard him mention it since—now that's impressive.

Coaching

strategy vs. tactics: Strategy relates to what you do well. To use a football analogy, the Green Bay Packers back in the '60s had very few offensive plays but were dominant for years. That's because they were so good at execution that it didn't matter if their opponents knew what was coming. This made the strategy fairly simple.

Tactics enter in when your opponent starts to break down your strategy. Not everyone executes like the Green Bay Packers, so sometimes you have to adjust. That's what we call making tactical adjustments within your strategy. This is a skill like any other, and developing it takes time, practice, and lots of experience. This is helpful to know as a parent, because it will explain why your kid, who may look like they hit the ball better than their opponents, seems to have such a tough time winning matches. It's great if your kid can hit the ball well, but learning how to play the game is more than that; that takes an understanding of strategy and tactics.

fundamentals vs. style: Fundamentals are the things that everyone agrees are essential to success. In tennis, you have to hit the ball over the net and get it in the court more often than your opponent to win a point. This is true for every player at every level. Should you do that with two hands or one hand on the racquet? Should you use an extreme or conventional grip? Should you swing fast or hard? Slice or topspin? Should you play at the baseline or come to the net? I could go on. You get the idea. All these are examples of style: different ways that players play, depending on what works for them.

I once spent a whole weekend at a conference with some of the best coaches in the country debating the differences between fundamentals and style. We really struggled to find consensus. Here are a few things we agreed on: Players with good fundamentals all use a unit turn to prepare for forehands and backhands. They all have a consistent swing path. They all hit the ball consistently in their strike zones.

Good players do these fundamentals consistently well across the board. That being said, they still may look different based on their individual style. I hope that makes sense.

The reason it's important for you to know, as a parent, is that you need to make sure your kid develops good fundamentals (technically, mentally, tactically, and emotionally), but that doesn't necessarily mean they will look or play like everyone else. So if your kid gets beat by someone with a certain game style or a specific spectacular shot, that doesn't necessarily mean those are fundamental to success for your kid.

negative thoughts vs. positive counters: I've never met an athlete who didn't have to deal with negative thoughts caused by self-judgement, frustration, insecurity, or fear. Trust me: your kid will have to fight that battle sooner or later. There are a few things you can do to help. First, accept that negative thoughts will come. They should be expected; it means they care. There is nothing wrong with your kid if they struggle with negativity. Second, help them become aware of how negative thoughts impact performance adversely. Believe it or not, many kids have no idea. Next, have them practice positive replacements for those thoughts. Here's a typical exchange in clinic.

Kid: I suck.
Coach: Hey, what's going on with you today?
Kid: I can't hit a backhand, and I hate losing to all these people I should beat easily.

Coach: Well, I noticed on those last points that you didn't move well enough to get the ball in your strike zone. Could you shadow stroke once and show me how you would move to get the ball into your strike zone?

Kid: [Makes no comment but, eyeing the coach suspiciously, complies.]

Coach: That looks good. Do you think on the next three backhands, you could hit from that strike zone, aiming deep down the middle with net clearance three to five feet over the net?

You have to guide kids through this process. The goal is to *redirect their mind from negative, general thoughts to a positive, specific one* and you will have to practice this yourself. I'm still working on it daily after years of coaching and playing. The goal, of course, is for your kid to learn how to independently apply positive counters for an endless variety of negative thoughts. This will take awareness, willingness, and effort on everyone's part. It's a skill to be practiced like any other.

Miscellaneous

hot-button kid: A player who, for whatever reason, catches the attention or interest of another player and who draws out their passion for the game. The best way to explain this concept is through illustration. Here's a hypothetical but realistic example. Sixteen-year-old Pete is the best kid in the state in his age group. If Pete is at practice, you can be assured that Joey, who is close in level but not as highly ranked, will be there. Pete, then, due to his higher ranking and level, is a hot-button kid for Joey. Joey, nevertheless, is still a great practice partner for Pete. But Raul (who just moved into town from Mexico and has a cool accent) is slightly better than Pete and practices across town at the newly formed, exclusive *XYZ Tennis Program for the Above Average*. In hopes of getting to practice with Raul, Pete decides to train at *XYZ*. Raul is Pete's hot-button kid. This leaves Joey disoriented and discouraged when he shows up to practice with no Pete around. Meanwhile, upon arriving at XYZ, Pete realizes that Raul could care less about practicing with him. He's leaving next week to train at a full-time academy in Florida where the players are better and the coaches speak more Spanish. Most of the guys Pete gets to train with at XYZ are weaker players than Joey.

I know this may sound confusing—welcome to the world of junior sports. Bottom line for parents: it's great if your kid gets to play with their hot-button kids, but becoming obsessed with that is not in your, or their, best interest. Better to focus on the bigger picture and expect your kid to hold themselves to a high standard regardless of who they're practicing with. Jumping around in search of the hot button kids leads to enablement rather than independence.

APPENDIX 1

the cloud: If you take athletes in any sport and compare them over time relative to each other, you will find there is rarely one who consistently stands out. The superstars are easy to spot, but they are far and few between. Even the strongest players in any one group lose occasionally, struggle with their own weaknesses, or have trouble disciplining themselves mentally. And there's a wide range of skill levels that players exhibit over time. There's always overlap, the top few kids in a lower group, on any given day, are often just as good as the bottom few in the next highest group. The "cloud" is the overlap between one group and the next.

Whenever I hear the story about Michael Jordan getting cut from his high school basketball team, I think of this concept. I empathize with the coach because he was dealing with the cloud. So if your kid reaches a milestone—getting picked for the team, moving up in clinic, winning a tournament, or beating their archrival—realize they were most likely in a cloud of people at about their same level. Let them bask in the feeling of satisfaction for a short time, but make sure they don't get complacent and lose touch with reality. If haven't yet reached that milestone moment, explain this concept to them so they realize they are never as far from reaching the goal as it may appear. The Michael Jordan example might be a good one to use—assuming, of course, that your kid knows who that is and you haven't used it too much in the past (as most coaches like myself have).

Stuff kids say

"I played terribly today": This is simply an example of a negative thought in need of a positive counter. It's the expression kids use when they lose or *feel* like they played poorly. Note: most kids who lose assume a direct correlation: if they win, they played well; if they lost, they played terribly. I've had countless interactions with kids who have concluded they were "playing terrible today" because they lost by one point against a great player in the first ten minutes of clinic. They are usually obsessed with the one easy shot they missed on the last point. Most likely, the reality was that they played well overall; it just didn't feel that way because they lost. Parents with competitively-wired kids will hear the "I played terrible today" line quite often. Keep in mind this is often based on emotion rather than reality. Good luck and stay patient; expecting competitive kids to understand this can take some time. I try to keep this in mind as a coach, since I was a poster child for the "I played terrible" school of thought as a player.

"There was no one there today": This is an example of a player who is overly focused on the hot-button kid concept (see above). At the clinic they have, no doubt, asked me a question like, "Where is everybody today?" or "Who else is coming today?" or "Why is nobody here?" There may have been twenty other kids in clinic, many of whom were perfectly reasonable practice partners, but that doesn't mean much if their own hot-button kids weren't around. I don't say this as a criticism of the kids; I would have thought the same thing at their age. I mention it because I've known a few parents who buy into this concept, compulsively hanging around after they drop their kids off to see which other kids show up, which group their kid is in, what court they're on, and so on. But, as I've hopefully brought out in this book, one of the main benefits of sports is that you learn character traits that enable you to excel under less than perfect conditions. If your kid gets the idea that practice conditions are only right if all the "right" people are around, they are being conditioned to focus on externals rather than internals. This is not good.

"Clinic was fun": Like so many of the expressions your kid will have, this one has a lot to do with their wiring. If they are competitive, this means they won. If they are performance-oriented, it means they got to play fun games. If they are relational, it means their friends were there that day. All this is perfectly normal for the kids.

I would caution, though, that you, as a parent, not to get too excited either way. Sooner or later, your kid will have a clinic, tournament, or practice that wasn't so fun. This doesn't mean anything was wrong with the experience; it just means the conditions I listed weren't met perfectly in your kid's mind. And it's important that your kid realizes, better sooner than later, that life isn't perfect all the time.

If you're competitive and you lost, you have to learn how to deal with that. If you're performance-oriented and you didn't get to play your favorite games, figure out a way to enjoy the ones you did get to play. If you're relational and your friend wasn't there that day, learn how to make new friends. This pretty much sums up one of the themes of this book: sports provide a great environment for kids to develop character, learn life skills, and build relationships.

Appendix 2:
An Email from the Dark Side

The email you are about to read was forwarded by another coach requesting that I "look at this and help me figure out where to start. I only have an hour a week with him. Help! Please." It represents an extreme example of how far down the path a sports parent can go—in the wrong direction. I hesitate to include it here. I don't want to vilify this, or any, parent. But I have to admit that when I spot similar mindsets in the parents of kids I coach, I have the urge to run in the opposite direction. I try to keep in mind, though, that they simply know not what they are doing. First the email, followed by what I'll call observations, solutions, and conclusions.

Hi.

I am sending you the last 2 match play results. There are a few things he really needs to work on.

My biggest worry is that he is no longer playing aggressively and controlling the match. He is always playing defense and hitting off his heels. He has opportunities to take control of the point and he doesn't drive it, he just gets it back. Don't really know why his game has changed so much, but it's not a good thing. he needs more energy during the match.

Return of serve—misses too many consistently. Each game he returned was a 40-0 or 40-15 game. He can't get the balls back. When he does there is nothing on it and his opponent hits a winner.

A few things were happening throughout all the matches. 1st serve was bad—he hit the net way too much. Don't know if his toss is wrong or he's not snapping his wrist. I do know he was dropping his left arm too fast on the ones going in the net.

When pulled off the court, he throws up a lob every time to the middle of the court and the person will come in and hit a volley or midcourt ball for a winner. I want him to learn how to get to the ball and hit a groundstroke. Sometimes he has no choice but others he could have gotten there and tried to hit it. It became a really bad pattern.

When he would hit an angle shot from the inside of the court, it never had enough pace to be a winner and would come back most of the time for a winner for the other person.

He needs to take the balls out of the air. He didn't do it one time the whole tournament. Please make this happen. I told him he needed to be doing this by the next tournament. Everyone else is doing it and it ends the point—he can too.

APPENDIX 2

He needs to drive the ball instead of brushing up on the ball. Not enough pace. In order for him to beat these players, he needs to hit pace down the line. He aims too close to the line and it usually goes out— esp. on forehand. I think his racquet head speed can be increased and it'll help with this tremendously. Hopefully his new racquets will too.

He is right on the edge. These guys are spending twice as many hours on the court as he is, and he is hanging with them. He's close. Unfortunately, he always makes it close in the first set and goes away in the second???

He gets another cortisone shot next week, so maybe he can lay off the backhand some this week.

Ok, you've got your work cut out for you.

Observations

- I mentioned back in the preface my dad's criticism of my lack of hustle on and off the baseball field, even though I had played great during the game. His intent, I'm certain, was to encourage me to push myself. The unintended result was that I developed a perfectionistic approach toward sports, which caused problems later in life. This email brought back that memory. This parent was focused almost totally on the problems with his kid, not at all on positives. I was certain this would have a negative impact on his kid long-term. Even if we could get the kid to improve in the areas in which his dad *perceived* to be lacking—defensive play, inconsistent returns, dropping his left arm too fast on serves, and so on— I'm certain he would simply come up with a new list and repeat this hypercritical, negative cycle? Responding to his requests would be like putting a band aid on a cut that needed stitches. This is a tough spot to be in if you're a tennis pro.

- Just about every problem this dad points to—"no longer playing aggressively," "playing defense," "hitting off his heels," and so on—describes a player who is afraid to make mistakes. It's clear that this kid is playing *not to lose* rather than playing to win. He knows he's constantly being evaluated and, therefore, playing out of a sense of fear rather than challenge. *To learn to play aggressively, you have to be given the freedom to fail.* I'm certain the last thing this player associates with his parent is freedom. Instead, he is controlled by the fear of making mistakes. The parent seems to have no awareness of this principle or that he is contributing to the problem off the court, which is why he can't understand his kid's inability to execute what "needs" to be done on the court.

- If you put yourself in the position of the player who is the subject of this critique, you can see how discouraging it might be. First, it's way too detailed. There is no way a player could possibly hope to address all these issues, concerns, and problems. Second, the tone is quite negative and general. Terms like "he is always," "he can't," "every time," "didn't do it 1 time the whole tournament," and "everyone else" are peppered throughout. At best, *a kid in this situation would simply tune out their parent as a coping mechanism. At worst, they would either rebel or burnout and quit altogether.*

- Clearly this parent has some working knowledge of and/or experience with the sport. I'm sure many of his observations were on target. But knowledge can be a dangerous thing, especially in the world of sports parenting, because it can lead to paralysis through analysis. Therefore his feedback, albeit well intentioned, may have some use for the coach but was essentially irrelevant for the player. *When you give someone too much information, it has the same effect as giving them none.*

- This email is a great example of *a parent's need for an awareness of the dichotomies and concepts discussed in this book.* Clearly this parent was too deeply involved in his kid's tennis, and as a result, it's doubtful the kid had any sense of ownership (enablement vs. independence). There's an urgency in tone (sprint vs. marathon), an unproductive focus on others (comparison vs. character), and a lack of sensitivity towards wiring (competitive, performance, relational). The wiring of this dad is obvious: direct, clear, confident, competitive. But had he considered the wiring of his kid? Or was he just operating based on what felt right to him (inclinations vs. effectiveness)?

Solutions

- An email like this one can be healthy if it's used by the parent as a way to vent. So it's better shared with the coach rather than the player. Parents can be a great resource for coaches. After all, they know their kids much better than we do as coaches. The biggest problem I had in this case was that the email seemed to dictate rather than defer—"please make this happen" rather than "what do you think?" The parent was already playing the role of the coach; he just wanted someone else to execute his vision—"ok you've got your work cut out for you." But it's better to *look at the parent-coach relationship as a partnership.* Earlier in this book I used the example of a dad who had similar inclinations toward overinvolvement and detail. I explained that getting into the weeds at ground level wouldn't be his best use of time and energy; he needed to fly at thirty thousand feet and focus on the big picture. I suggested that whenever he needed to vent about details, he write it up in an email and send it to me. He told me that he sensed his natural inclinations might have some unintended negative side effects, so my suggestion was well received. Fortunately he trusted my judgement and knew I would follow up on his suggestions when appropriate. That way his concerns were usually resolved without his direct intervention. This, to me, was a great example of the benefits of a parent-coach partnership.

- A better way to approach this would be *for the player to write up his own analysis and communicate with the coach directly.* If the parent was copied in on that exchange, he would likely find that his kid was already aware of most of the issues, which would, hopefully, have eased his mind somewhat. Most kids won't use as many words and may miss a few details, but that's a great trade-off, because both the parent and coach can gauge the player's understanding and then work from there. This email seems to assume total cluelessness on the part of the player. It's doubtful that's the case. Either way, it doesn't matter if the parent has clarity on what needs to be done or how to do it. All that matters is what the player understands, can execute, and is committed to doing.

- It would be helpful if this parent could *learn how to replace broad, negative generalities* (always, never, can't) *with positive, actionable specifics* (focus on this, execute that, try to do this). This is really the essence of good coaching. Since parents are often with kids at tournaments, sometimes getting pulled into the role of coach, this is a good skill to have. Players perform best with positive, specific cues in the moment. And they need to learn how to replace their own negative thoughts with positive counters. One of the best things a parent can do is learn how to model this for their kid. It takes awareness, emotional discipline, and lots of practice for all concerned.

- For parents who occasionally find themselves in a coaching role, I would suggest the following grid. Start by thinking about *purpose*. Are you saying this because you are frustrated, angry, or disappointed? Or will this be constructive feedback that your kid will be willing and able to act on? Second, think about *content*. What do you really want to say? Particularly if you have a long list of issues/concerns (as this dad did), try to be clear and concise. Third, be mindful of your *delivery*; how you say it can have just as much impact as what you say. Lastly, remember that *timing* is important. Sometimes coaching feedback is best delivered immediately, but sometimes it's best to wait awhile. Figuring all this out takes effort because like most relationships, coaching is often more art form than science. It requires an awareness of your kid's age, temperament, and emotional maturity. It also requires empathy and self-control on your part.

- It's rarely difficult to find things a player needs to do better; the real challenge is to *narrow things down and design a realistic plan* with timelines, goals, specific drills, and practice schedules. There are four interconnected areas of the game: physical, technical, strategic, and emotional. Anyone with even a little knowledge of the sport can usually find at least one or two areas from each category to be addressed. This can get complicated very quickly. The secret is to simplify things for players by deciphering the key fundamental issues that tend to mitigate the others. It takes expertise to identify those issues and discipline to stay focused on only those. This is where good coaches can be invaluable. When I coach private lessons, I keep a file for each student divided into those four categories. When I start to work with a player, I collaborate with the player and sometimes with their parent to come to some agreement on the main areas that need to be addressed. We try to stay focused on those areas for three months and then reevaluate. Particularly for kids who play a lot of tournaments, this can be challenging, because there's a tendency to bounce around based on what problems arose in the last tournament (this email would be a good example from a parent's perspective). Better to go an inch wide and a mile deep and get real improvement than an inch deep and a mile wide and get none.

- Make a point to *be positive and encouraging without qualification*. It's easy to fall into a passive-aggressive dynamic that leaves kids feeling conflicted, confused, and discouraged. There is one point toward the end of this email where this parent did give some semblance of encouragement: "He is right on the edge. . . . He's close." Sadly that was immediately followed by more negative/general comments: "Unfortunately, he always makes it close in the first set and goes away in the second???" If you put yourself in the player's position, this would likely be crushing to your spirit. Just when your parent, the person you look to most for encouragement and support, gives you some ray of hope, they immediately follow it by stressing your flaws and shortcomings. Sometimes it's best simply to affirm courage, effort, and character and leave it at that.

Conclusions

- There will be no real fix for the player here unless the elephant in the room is addressed: the parent's mindset. Success in training a puppy lies not just in the expertise but with the energy of the trainer. Stressed out, undisciplined trainers end up with stressed out, undisciplined dogs. It's the same in sports parenting. Unless the parent understands this, there really isn't anything of lasting substance the tennis pro can bring to the table. There might be some short-term improvement in a few areas, but the dysfunctional environment will continue to limit progress. My hope is that parents who recognize themselves in this email, even if not to such an exaggerated level, would see the *need to break the cycle of negativity.* Maybe the principles in this book can serve as a starting point for that. If not, my conclusion as a coach would be to do the best I could with the player, put up with the parent, and hope for the best. It's when I apply the traditional prayer about having the serenity to accept the things you can't change, courage to change the things you can, and wisdom to know the difference.

- At this stage, this player (and parent) would need a full-time coach rather than a part-time pro. The issues that need to be addressed would require a lot of work with the parent off-court, not to mention many hours on-court with the player. In this case, the pro had one hour per week with the player, which is barely enough time to scratch the surface. Paying a pro hourly wouldn't get the job done. It would be better to hire a coach on a retainer to: work multiple hours per week with the player, spend time with the parent off the court, and attend some tournaments. Unfortunately, this would be an unrealistic option for most families. Better for the parent to get clued in earlier on how to be a good sports parent. As in most things, *a little effort on the front end precludes lots of challenges on the back end.*

- Many kids brought up in this hypercritical, overinvolved environment become highly-ranked juniors and often go on to play college tennis, since their parents make sure they are provided every opportunity. But this often comes with lots of emotional and physical baggage. They rarely reach their potential due to mental burnout, lack of ownership, limited passion for the game, or injury due to overuse (note this parents last comment, "he gets another cortisone shot next week", yikes!). After having their parents as a crutch when they were juniors, they find it hard to learn to walk on their own in college. Ironically, *the parents who disconnect somewhat from the on-court details often end up with the most successful kids on and off the court.*

For example, my friend John was a highly-ranked junior in North Carolina. Toward the end of his junior career, he qualified for the Southern Closed, a prestigious event involving players from all over the south. The event was to be held in another state hours away. Excited at that prospect he asked if he could go, hoping that his dad might volunteer to take him. His dad didn't see the value in traveling hours to play a tennis tournament. Particularly considering the time and money involved, the fact that John had a summer job, and that he was preparing for college the next fall (John was going to Duke where, I suspect, his dad figured John's tennis pursuits would fade into the background). Undaunted, John arranged for time off from his summer job and a ride to the tournament with a friend whose parent was driving. (For what it's worth, most tennis parents I've known whose kids qualify for that tournament eagerly support and facilitate their kids playing the event, no questions asked.) Having taken care of the details himself, John approached his dad again and got permission to go. That tournament turned out to be a key to his development, as it exposed John to higher level competition and gave him the confidence to make the tennis team at Duke (where he played for four years and got a great education). I would argue that his dad was a great tennis parent, precisely because he had the big picture in mind and didn't get immersed in the details. John, in turn, developed the initiative and discipline to pursue his goals on his own. I think that experience was a test of John's character, well-orchestrated by his dad. Once John passed that test, his dad was not only supportive but, I'm certain, quite proud.

Finally . . .

I hope the email above was written in the heat of the moment and that neither the content nor spirit was shared by this parent with his kid. Either way, I include it here for a few reasons. First, as an illustration of how detailed and critical parents can get; second, as an example of how easily the line between parenting and coaching can be crossed; and lastly, as a warning that it if you go down a similar path, you can easily get where this parent seemed to be—a stressed out bundle of frustration, impatience, and overinvolvement—none of which, in my opinion, served much purpose.

Appendix 3:

Short Answers to Big Questions

Chapter 1: Why Is Sports Parenting So Hard? (Inclinations vs. Effectiveness)

Sports parenting is hard because:

- it requires balancing a host of dichotomies, such as control and freedom, proactive and reactive, aggressive and passive, commission and omission;
- the culture of sports heightens everyone's emotions, particularly those of parents, making it hard to maintain perspective and make good decisions;
- there is no single approach that guarantees success; the only thing that's constant is change;
- by the time you have it figured out, it's over.

Chapter 2: How Do I Coach My Kid? (Plans vs. Principles)

Coach your kid by:

- understanding yourself as a "team leader," not a coach—there's a difference;
- focusing more on flying at thirty thousand feet than walking at ground level—don't sweat the small stuff;
- realizing that your passion for the sport may not be shared by your kid—give them the freedom to find that passion on their own (or not to);

- establishing principles that will guide your behavior rather than relying on one plan you think will insure success.

Chapter 3: How Do We Choose the Right Coach/Program? (Form vs. Substance)

Choose the right coach/program by:
- seeking out a program that provides a good learning environment for all the kids, not just the "best" kids;
- deciding whether you are looking for a pro or a coach—it's helpful to make that distinction;
- finding coaches who love coaching, communicate honestly with parents, are stable emotionally, and who exhibit professionalism;
- looking for character, competence, consistency, and caring; what coaches say and do matters, but who they are as people matters more

Chapter 4: How Do "We" Get to the Next Level? (Outcome vs. Process)

Get to the next level by:
- Understanding that how kids practice is more important than who they're practicing with.
- Encouraging your kid to do the things other kids aren't doing; good news, this shouldn't cost you anything.

- Keeping the wins and losses in perspective; they're never as good as their best day, nor as bad as their worst. The goal is continual improvement rather than achieving one outcome.

Chapter 5: What Should I Know about Competition? (Competition vs. Character)

You should:
- be aware of your "wiring" and how it compares to your kids;
- focus on your circle of influence: you and your kid;
- resist the temptation to compare your kid to others, and look at competition as an opportunity for your kid to develop character;
- learn to see the forest rather than just the trees; the things that really matter usually aren't evident in the moment.

Chapter 6: Do I Have to Be as Intense as the Other Parents? (Sprint vs. Marathon)

What you have to do is:
- educate yourself, set realistic expectations, and act according to what's best for you;
- set a pace you can sustain over the long term—intense parents create environments that often lead to dysfunction and burnout;

- focus on principles that help you run the marathon rather than get caught up in the moment;
- remember that if you want your kid learn how to control their emotions, you have to set the standard.

Chapter 7: Will This Be Worth the Effort? (Enablement vs. Independence)

Definitely. But:

- encourage responsibility and ownership so they can succeed independent of you—that's worth whatever time, money, and effort you put in;
- realize that the worthwhile lessons are often learned through failure; sometimes it's best to give them the freedom to discover those lessons on their own;
- understand that the payoff is in non-tangibles (life skills, character development, and relationships) rather than a financial return on investment;
- remember that the goal is to build capable, productive members of society; sports are simply one of the means to that end.

Acknowledgements

Thanks to the countless parents who have entrusted their kids to me over the years. Some have challenged me to my limits (which is why I started writing this book years ago). But many have inspired, encouraged, and supported me in countless ways. I've tried to do my best with all your kids, especially on the tough days.

Thanks also to both of my parents, Anna and Bill Schillings, whose impact continues to be felt long after they are gone - in my life, the lives of our family, and, hopefully, the lives of the parents and players I've influenced through coaching.

To two special men who have inspired me to be a better coach and human being. Terry McMahon, my high school coach who impacted me beyond description as a teenager and continues to influence me to this day. Where you finish is determined by how strong your foundation was when you started. I couldn't have found a better coach, advocate, mentor, and role model in my formative years. What a blessing to still be able to share life with you. And to Peter Daub, my tennis coach after college. How fortunate I was that you crossed my path so many years ago. You made me into a better a tennis player, provided opportunities for me in life, mentored me in business, but, most importantly, have been a rare and valuable friend . . . the kind who loves you enough to always tell the truth, even when it's hard to hear. I've tried to pay forward what you guys have taught and modeled for me. This book is one example of that.

Thanks to Barry Hudock for editing, Eva Crawford for help with cover art, and Pender Murphy for writing the foreword. And a very special thanks to my daughters - Kara, who proofread this manuscript during nap times for Wren, and Kristin, who was my beta reader throughout the writing of this book – love you two more than words can say.

And last but never least, thanks to my lovely wife Elizabeth Jean Marie Bonino Schillings without whom this book, nor anything of consequence in my life, would have ever happened. You're my favorite.

About the author

After graduating from Penn State University where he was captain and played #1 in singles and doubles, Bill Schillings competed on the professional tennis tour both in the United States and abroad. He then served as an assistant tennis coach at Temple University, where he received his MA in sports administration.

Bill is a USTA High Performance Coach, USPTA Elite Professional, and was recognized as the NCTA 2016 Tennis Professional of the Year. He owned and directed Charlotte Tennis Academy from 1989-2022 where he coached and mentored countless juniors…and occasionally their parents. His observations and reflections on what made for successful sports parenting became the inspiration for this book.

Bill and his wife Liz live in Charlotte, North Carolina. They are the proud parents of two amazing daughters who have grown to become independent, capable, and well-balanced members of society.

www.ingramcontent.com/pod-product-compliance
Lightning Source LLC
LaVergne TN
LVHW012020060526
838201LV00061B/4391